Not in Front of the Servants

Not in Front of the Servants

HUMOUR WITH CLASS

DEREK NIMMO

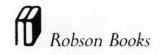

Robson Books

The author and publishers are grateful to the proprietors of
Punch magazine for permission to include *Punch* cartoons in
this book, to John Murray Ltd and the executors of the
late Sir Osbert Lancaster for permission to include those on
pp 76 and 157, and to ABP for the Thelwell cartoon on
p 155.

First published in Great Britain in 1987 by Robson Books
Ltd, Bolsover House, 5−6 Clipstone Street, London W1P
7EB.

British Library Cataloguing in Publication Data

Nimmo, Derek
 Not in front of the servants.
 I. Title
 828′.91407   PN6175
ISBN 0−86051−446−3

Printed in Great Britain by Billing & Sons Ltd., Worcester.

Contents

To John Cawston

Introduction

For a recent *Sunday Times* Colour Supplement, I was invited to feature with one of my children in an article entitled 'Relatively Speaking'. The point of the series is that children should talk in a candid way about their parents and vice versa. Although I was quite happy to chat about any of my children, I was distinctly nervous as to what they might say about me. I remembered that years before, during my temporary absence from the family home, an enterprising reporter from the *Daily Mail* had managed to persuade the children's nanny to allow her an interview with my then small son, Timothy. When I returned home and learnt of this intrusion, I quizzed him closely about what he had said. 'Oh I can't remember, Daddy,' was his distinctly unhelpful reply. For the next few days, I perused my *Daily Mail* with increasing anxiety. About a week later, there was a teaser on the front page which read, 'My Father's a Twit' by Timothy Nimmo.

With some frenzy, I pulled the paper apart until I found the offending article. It really wasn't quite so bad. 'My Father's a Twit, but a very nice Twit. There's a lot of money in being a Twit and I'd like to be a Twit when I grow up.'

Well he has grown up and is certainly not a Twit, but I felt with some reason that it might be injudicious to give him a second chance to comment upon his Pa. After all these years he might not prove to be quite so charitable.

My daughter, Amanda, was a different matter. I thought that she, at least, might be loyal and, at the same time, sufficiently discreet as not to reveal the full awful truth about me to the gentle readers of the *Sunday Times*.

Amanda did not really disappoint me. Her appraisal was pleasantly fictional as well as being decidedly flattering. That is, until the last paragraph.

I thought, until I reached it, that I had experienced a miraculous escape. I then read, 'My Father is a snob'. Alas it didn't go on to read, 'But a very nice snob', or even, 'There's a lot of money in being a snob', etc, etc, just, 'My Father is a snob'. Was I really? I pondered.

Snobbery, I had read, was considered to be the behaviour of inferior people, aping, or trying to achieve an acquaintanceship with, those higher up the social ladder than they are.

Again I thought. Was I really like that?

The English have always been considered, by foreigners, to be the most snobbish people in the world. With some justification, I suppose. In the past, you could always put two Englishmen together and by their use of certain key words and phrases, they would rapidly decide upon the other's social positions. This has, however, been made more confusing by such learned writers as Nancy Mitford, Professor Alan S.C. Ross, Donald Sutherland, Richard Buckle – not forgetting the tasty Jilly Cooper. As a result of their published researches, shoals of perfectly happy, previously socially secure citizens were, overnight, made to reassess their vocabulary and move upmarket from 'mantelpiece, toilet and serviette' to 'chimneypiece, loo and table napkin'. Had I been one of these? I had certainly always used a 'mirror' until the good professor advised me that 'looking glass' was more acceptable.

Did I really only start saying 'flog' for 'sell' when Richard Buckle revealed that the Earl of Pembroke had pronounced it 'oojah-cum-spiff'?

Is the changed appearance of my window-box this summer due to the fact that Jilly Cooper decreed that Cambridge Blue lobelia is OK but Oxford Blue is common?

I certainly had no excuse for snobbery as I am boringly middle-class, but then I suppose the more middle-class you are, the more prone you can be to snobbery. The working class are totally confident in their social status, as indeed are the aristocracy. It is the great floundering mass in the middle that are insecure. All those looking with envy to those above them in the pecking order and with disdain to those they imagine to be beneath. An epitaph for A.E. Housman recorded that he was the only member of the middle-classes who never called himself a gentleman.

That, then, is perhaps why my daughter called me a snob. I have always lived with some tiny hope of becoming, if not being, a gentleman; an ambition fuelled by once reading, 'There are times when one can forgive a man almost anything if he has the essential attributes of a gentleman.' And what are these attributes? All, I think, pretty good ones: courtesy, chivalry, consideration, an unwritten but instantly recognizable code of behaviour that makes our living together on this increasingly bewildering planet, slightly more tolerable. Much more complex than my mother's definition of a gentleman, which is simply, 'A man who uses the butter knife when he is by himself.' She was, and is, greatly concerned with the outward trappings of good breeding, such as leaving undone the bottom button of one's waistcoat, the raising of hats, offering one's seat to a lady, etc, etc. In spite of this veneer, maternally imposed, I have always had a sneaking fear that I was, in truth, what my mother again would disparagingly denounce as 'not quite a gentleman'.

It was a remark of the late Lord Arran that confirmed my worst suspicions. He once said, 'If you see somebody driving a Rolls Royce, you know he's not a gentleman – unless he's the chauffeur.' Now, I have driven myself in a progression of Rolls Royces and Bentleys over some twenty-five years. Was this where I failed? Obviously, I decided, I must take a back seat and the sooner the better. It was then that Cawston came into my life. He is the rather gloomy old cove whose snapshot you will see on the cover of this book. I had known, or rather spoken to, him for many years. He used to own a company in Knightsbridge called John's Personal Services, and if you ever needed extra staff for a dinner party, a quick call to JPS would send them tripping round. But now my requirements were different. Having read the damning words of Buffy Arran I knew I was in terminal need of a chauffeur. I called John Cawston and told him of my plight.

'I see, sir,' said the frightfully grand voice at the other end of the telephone. 'What colour livery would you require him to wear, sir?'

That stumped me. 'H … h … h … How do you mean?' I said.

'What is the colour of your Rolls Royce, motor car, sir?'

'Oh, I s … s … see. Well, it's a rather nasty brown beneath and the top bit is a sort of cream leather. Well,

I suppose it's plastic, really.'

'Goodness gracious me, sir! Is that so, sir?' The disdain in his voice showed that he regarded me as totally beyond several pales for not only having hitherto driven the car myself but also for having what is known in the trade as 'a two-tone car.'

'I will endeavour to meet your requirements, sir.'

The next day, a tall, thin chap turned up at my house. He was wearing dark brown jackboots, cream jodhpurs and a chocolate brown double-breasted tunic resplendent with gleaming crested buttons. He matched the car perfectly, right down to the hub caps. He touched where his forelock would have resided in earlier years. 'I hope I can be of assistance, sir.'

Assistance? This was Cawston himself, and the man proved to be indispensable. He is like a quick-change artist in some exotic cabaret. At the drop of his peaked cap, he will transform into a butler or footman. He has a wardrobe of the grandest liveries all bearing *his* family crest. I've known him change his frock three times in one evening. Once when collecting some friends who were having dinner at my house, he first appeared in a black livery with white gloves. He then bobbed up at the dinner table playing a footman and he then ran them home in a third, rather natty, light grey livery. Next day I received a telephone call from one of our rattled guests enquiring whether I employed triplets!

I don't think, however, that observing Lord Arran's dictum and sitting in the stern has made me feel any more of a gentleman – rather the reverse. Cawston (Downside and Cambridge) is so hugely smart; the epitome of an English would-be-gentleman's gentleman. I now sit slumped in the back of my grey car (Cawston made me get rid of the other one rather speedily) while he drives, regaling me the while with stories located both Upstairs and Downstairs. I play a very suburban Bertie Wooster to this most imperious of Jeeves. Through listening to Cawston's sundry scurrilous stories, I got the idea for this book.

Did I tell you, sir, about a house party that I was at in Wiltshire in 39? Well, one of the guests, a frightfully pretty young gairl (sic), now the Marchioness of ———, was cautioned before retiring about the sexual proclivities of a certain belted earl, who was a member of the same house party. Having received the warning, she was then advised to lock her door firmly when she went to her room.

Sure enough, soon after getting into bed, sir, she heard three loud knocks on the door.

Obeying her host's instruction, she stayed in her room and said not a word. A little later the knocks came once more. Again, she did not stir. Then they came a third time, accompanied by a voice saying, 'If you knew what I was knocking on the door with, you would let me in.'

What do you imagine it was, sir? A small Cartier box?

Well, that obviously is a story I cannot put in the book. However, I hope you will enjoy the others that Cawston has allowed me to include. I have chosen them because, in the main, they are curiously British stories, only understood by the fellow countrymen that I mentioned earlier who spend so much time trying to climb a curiously unimportant social ladder.

There are also a number of tales of eccentrics and eccentricities. This was inevitable, for, as has been well documented, the English aristocracy has spawned per capita over the years more than its fair share.

A couple of weeks ago I paid a visit to the dowager Lady Selby at her mews cottage near Harrods. To my surprise, on the cobbles, acting as a doorstep to the house was a much thumbed copy of *Debrett's Peerage*.

'Veronica, what's this doing here?' I enquired.

'Oh, darling, really! The children have got to know from where they came!'

That now, come to think of it, is a story that I could have included. I know that Cawston would have approved. Upon reflection I cannot imagine why I chose *Not in Front of the Servants* as the title for this book. Cawston knows much juicier tales than I will ever hear. I hope he will put them on paper one day – *Not in Front of the Master,* perhaps? Now, he really is a snob . . .

BREEDING
SHOWS

Learning our place in society is one of those uncomfortable lessons some of us are taught alarmingly early in our three score years and ten.

Witness the case of the baby boy born to a Scots couple within a thane's cry of Glamis Castle, who found himself, barely into his first fresh nappy, saddled with the birth registration number thirteen – and all in the line of royal duty. Princess Margaret happened to have been born at more or less the same time and to spare her the indignity of the baker's dozen, this poor little chap had to carry the can.

Even more galling must have been watching his mother's enthusiasm and delight at being able to offer her son for this small service. The only possible consolation might have been the faint hope that this served as the first step in acquiring that natural dignity summed up by a comment of Edmund Burke's, 'Somebody has said, that a king may make a nobleman, but he cannot make a gentleman' – but it's pretty cold comfort.

The little princess's grandfather, King George V, might have gleaned an inkling of what Burke was driving at from a telling exchange with one of his grandsons near the end of his life. Coming across the little boy engrossed in a book, the old king asked what he was reading. 'It's a history book,' he was told.

'And who are you studying?' asked the grandfather.

'Perkin Warbeck.'

'And who was he?'

'He's just someone who pretended he was the son of a king. But he wasn't really; he was the son of respectable parents.'

Now, here the young prince hit on one of the corner-stones on which the distinction between the gentleman and everyone else has been laboriously built – respectability.

Up and down the social ladder parents have been striving to maintain this throughout history. Today it takes a variety of forms from the latest gleaming model fresh from the production lines of Dagenham or Yokohama, to the ritual display of a cracked and chipped Derby dinner service as a brave reminder of times lost and gone for ever.

For almost every parent there's the ever-present question of how best to raise their offspring – and here changes have been afoot in the cradle and classroom.

Many years ago now *The Lady* picked up a growing trend among what it chose to call 'young mothers of the aristocratic and cultivated sorts' who were completely breaking with tradition and actually undertaking to bring up their babies themselves, though it was pointed out reassuringly that they weren't complete novices, having been 'expert and successful in the raising and training of animals'.

Dark hints about the decline of the middle classes were given thirty years ago by one Lieutenant-Colonel Bromley-Davenport, who reported that along with having to cash in their investments, move to smaller houses and generally wave goodbye to their accepted independence, many middle-class parents were even being reduced to sending their children to state schools.

This quickening breeze of social democracy hasn't

met with universal enthusiasm. Those who recall the palmy days when children were seen and not heard, one of the principal doctrines in the rearing of young gentlemen and ladies, view these developments with a somewhat jaundiced eye. Children today enjoy a spoken wisdom well in advance of their years.

'And what are you going to do, dear, when you're as big as your mummy,' an elderly friend asked a little girl whose family she was visiting. 'Diet,' answered the child.

The general demise of nannies and top-floor nurseries has frequently led to children gate-crashing evening entertainments formerly the exclusive preserve of their seniors. One wretched hostess of a large country house party found herself landed with a precocious eight-year-old who refused to be diverted by her son's computer games or the Sylvester Stallone video they'd hired specially for the occasion, and had to resort to giving the child a conducted tour of the house to salvage her carefree gathering. Entering the library, where she hoped to dump the brat, she was horrified to discover two of her guests cavorting naked in front of the fire. 'Mending the hearth-rug – how thoughtful,' she remarked, hurriedly ushering the child out again. Now, in the old days that wouldn't have happened; nor would the business in front of the fire for that matter.

Glasnost may be all very well around international conference tables but it can play havoc with well-ordered family meals. 'You mustn't stare at Uncle Peter,' whispered an anxious mother to her small son whose eyes were fixed on the ruddy-complexioned man seated across the lunch table. 'But I don't understand, Mummy,' piped up the child with penetrating clarity, 'I don't think he drinks like a fish.' (It's children like this who are just as likely to proffer a tumbler full of crème de menthe when a parent, harassed by Christmas guests, tells him to get the same merry uncle another drink.)

Staying in Wiltshire on one occasion, Christopher Thynne told me a similar story of when he was young. The family had one relation with a particularly large, protuberant nose, with whom he was invited with his siblings, as small children, to take tea. Strict instructions were given that on no account was the nose to be mentioned and all went well, with no reference being made to their relative's distinctive feature. Christopher's mother was tremendously relieved as disaster had been averted, but such was her confusion that she turned to their host and said, 'I'm so sorry, I was forgetting to ask you. Do you take nose with your tea?'

Then there's the difficulty caused by famous faces and features. When my elder son Timothy was at Wellington College he was wandering along one day in his usual vague way when a large, flag-ridden Rolls Royce, bearing Field Marshal Lord Montgomery of Alamein stopped. Monty leant out of the window and said to the small boy, 'Can you tell me the way to the Master's Lodge?'

Timothy gave the directions and when he'd finished, Montgomery asked, 'What's your name, boy?'

'Nimmo, sir,' was the reply.

'Are you any relation to that actor fellow?'

'Yes, sir, he's my father.'

'Oh,' said Montgomery. 'Do you know who I am?'

Timmy then said, 'Yes, I've seen you on television lots of times.'

This was a story that the Field Marshal repeated

with great glee as soon as he reached the Master's residence.

Seen from the other side, the situation can be a little less good humoured in the classroom. I recall the experience of the young son of an actor chum who soon tired of his fame at nursery school. 'And whose little boy are you?' he'd be asked by visiting adults, to whom he'd been pointed out by members of staff. That was until the day when his patience cracked, and he snapped back at an unwary enquirer, 'You know exactly who I am!'

It's probably an attempt to nip in the bud awkward tendencies of this sort that lead so many parents to hark back to what they fondly perceive as past values; to mortgage themselves for a decade or two into the future, and to go knocking at the doors of status, privilege and, of course, respectability – the prep and public schools.

Not that these have escaped change. According to an advertisement that appeared in the middle of the last century those charged with the care of pupils at even a small prep school had very specific and exacting duties. The lucky candidate (in this case a young lady) was kept well occupied:

> She must be able to instruct them in reading, spelling, writing and the rudiments of history and geography. She will be expected to give her constant attention to the children; and, as the manners and deportment of young boys are matters of importance, it is requisite that she shall have moved in genteel society.

Her other duties included: washing twenty-five

faces and as many pairs of hands every morning (the servants washed the feet once a week), combing twenty-five heads with a small-tooth comb every Saturday, cutting 250 toenails, taking her charges to church twice on Sunday and supervising their prayers every morning. For this she received twenty-five guineas a year and was rewarded with three weeks off in the summer.

Just over a century later *The Times Educational Supplement* carried an advertisement that laid rather different emphasis on the prerequisites of the teacher by seeking,

> Active public school Oxbridge man required in September, capable of coaching rugger, cricket, boys 8 to 18 years. Academic subjects unimportant but geography preferred. Ample scope for mountain activities.

Aside from the desirability of geography teaching, the two would appear to have little in common and yet both were carefully tailored to nurturing young gentlemen.

This raises questions about the whole purpose of the public school and the ethic it seeks to advance. Someone has sagely commented, 'public schools aren't for the sons of gentlemen, they're for the fathers of gentlemen', and judging by the elaborate financial arrangements that many parents have to make in order to restore these 'old values', the words *capital punishment* take on a fresh but almost as terrifying meaning.

Somebody else once remarked, more from enthu-siasm than erudition, that Jesus Christ was the first

public school man, and this attitude still pervades the
cloisters and stony corridors of many leading schools.
The story is told of a candidate for the post of
headmaster at a Church of England prep school, who
took one look at the board of governors interviewing
him and went right off the job. 'If you did become
headmaster here,' asked one of them, 'what would be
your main aim in educating those boys?'

'My aim, sir, would be to turn them into Christian
gentlemen,' replied the candidate.

'Yes, yes, but what does that mean?'

'With which of those terms are you unfamiliar?'
came the reply that assured the post for someone else.
Others had very definite ideas of what was meant.

Back in the last century Beaumont College chal-
lenged Eton to matches in football and cricket, to
which Eton reputedly answered, 'Winchester we
know; Harrow we have heard of; but who are you?'

Beaumont's reply was, 'We now are what you once
were – a school for English Catholic gentlemen.'

Neville Lytton, the artist, old Etonian and Renais-
sance man who tells this story, also had very set ideas
on what a public school should aim to achieve. He was
a pupil at Eton at the end of the last century and
detected even then the first sinister murmurs of
accountability and relevance creeping into the time-
honoured syllabus with which any well-schooled
citizen of ancient Rome would have been perfectly at
home. Dismissing 'up-to-date thrusters (the buzz-
around, business sort)' with their books and theories
on how to achieve success, he asked,

But what is success to the true philosopher and
deep thinker? It is excellence that matters, and one

of the chief parts of excellence is style, and style is achieved by the energetic pursuit of useless things – 'Le style, c'est l'homme.'

(Today, regrettably, 'Le style' may also be but a short step from 'le bankruptcy' – but I add gall to the wine.)

Not that a classical education is without its virtues. A former chairman of Shell was asked by a critical interviewer why so many men with degrees in Greats or other classical schools had been appointed as senior executives. 'Because they sell more oil than anyone else,' he was told.

Latin and Greek instill a clarity of thought and expression too. During one of the last Seasons before the outbreak of the Second World War it was reliably reported that that year's debs were studying Greek philosophy to prepare them for their curtsies at Court. Apparently this was a valuable mental exercise.

Then there was a diner in a West End restaurant overheard not many years ago ordering a 'Martinus'.

'You mean a Martini, sir,' gently corrected the waiter.

'No – a Martinus,' persisted the diner. 'I was taught Latin properly and I only want one.'

Alas the same can't be said of the pupil, possibly a contemporary of the man in the restaurant, who translated 'Pax in bello' with an access of inspiration as 'Freedom from indigestion'.

I myself was never a great Latin scholar, mainly, I think, because I was so terrified of my classics master, one Fruity Williams. He had a favourite trick for when prospective parents were visiting the classroom, which was to invite me to stand up and conjugate my own name. The absolute horror of having to recite, 'Nimmo, nimmas, nimmat, nimmamas, nimmatis, nimmant' is with me still.

For many parents there are other anxieties inherent in their children's education besides those of the curriculum, though here again the upper echelons have a clearly laid out set of priorities. 'Few things – apart from war –' ran an article in *Cricketer*, 'can be more nerve-racking than the anxiety of a distinguished parent about the development of his son's cricket.'

Some forty years later the same publication reported the distressing case of two boys at Brighton College who had been suspended for disobedience that would have made any 'distinguished parent' throw up his hands in despair. They had chosen to revise for their imminent A-levels, rather than play in the Headmaster's cricket side against the Old Boys.

Parents (in most cases fathers) fondly imagine that their old schools are the final bastions of traditions they see fast disappearing from the world. No doubt it was that which led an old Etonian, who'd never touched water in his life, to send a barrel of beer to his son, so that he might be spared the indignity of drinking the water provided as sole beverage at his old house in a more 'enlightened' age.

In reality, just about the only factor that hasn't changed over the years is the problem of keeping pace with the increase in fees. Fifty years ago parents at Eton were complaining so loudly about the size of their sons' hat bills that the then headmaster, Mr Claude Elliott, had to issue a warning to lower boys against kicking and knocking about hats. Some of them, it seemed, were getting through three or four silk hats a term, at just over a pound a hat and at a time when a pound was a pound!

A parent's own appearance is of vital importance as well, leading an enterprising father to advertise once in *The Times* for a 'Sports car, preferably foreign, wanted week-end 22 June by respectable middle-aged civil servant, to raise son's status at preparatory school where most fathers have Jaguars.'

And what do they get in return for all this self-sacrifice? There are letters home, though not many, like this seasonal greeting from Christmas 1827:

Honoured parents,

As it is customary at this closing season of the year to honour our parents, our friends or our Guardians with a few lines written from school as a token of filial affection and gratitude, I have endeavoured to convince you that I am not unmindful of the parental solicitude and tenderness which you have bestowed on me during the state of my infancy and may I be able in maturer age, to express in stronger terms by my well ordered own conduct and show how grateful I feel, more especially from the advantage which must always accrue from an early education which I hope will be instrumental in promoting my temporal and eternal welfare. I trust that this short though affectionate tribute will be accepted as a substitute for a better, which I hope to offer in future life.

> I am, dear parents,
> Your most dutiful son,
> J. Joseph Greening

(Young master Greening was eleven years old when he penned this missive!)

The art of letter writing has declined since his day. My younger son, Piers, was just eight when he was sent to prep school for the first time. We missed him greatly and waited anxiously to receive the first letter from the Dragon. Eventually it arrived and we rushed to open it. There inside the letter started, 'Dear Mr and Mrs Nimmo . . .' My wife burst into floods of tears.

In 1940 the fond parents of a small boy away at boarding school received his dutiful Sunday letter and were surprised to see that it concluded after a few scanty lines with the message, 'I am afraid I must close now as the rest is of military importance.'

Staff too can be equally dismissive. The second master at one public school, sighting a group of women outside the headmaster's study, asked one of the porters, 'Who are those ladies waiting to see the headmaster?'

'Them's not ladies, sir,' replied the porter. 'Them's parents.'

So, why do parents struggle to pay the fees and keep up appearances in the name of respectability? Perhaps it has something to do with the comment of a mother who understood the reason all too clearly, when she summed up the difference between children of different backgrounds: 'Middle-class children take riding lessons and dancing lessons; lower-class children take anything that isn't nailed down.'

For the better off, paying for education doesn't end at school. Three (or more) years of parental contributions have to be found to supplement the maintenance grant and so send their brighter offspring to university. Mrs Thatcher may have remarked on the subject of student budgeting, 'I can't understand all the fuss about grants. Carol managed to save out of hers. Of course, we paid for her skiing holidays,' but many parents escape less lightly. Others don't even seek to.

Duncan Sandys's father presented his son with an Indian servant for his twenty-first birthday while he was still at Oxford.

Even after the war, well-heeled parents were setting up their student sons in the manner to which they were to become all too well accustomed. There was an advertisement in the *Worthing Gazette* seeking the services of an 'Experienced working cook-housekeeper, required for young bachelor University undergraduate's weekend luxury residence, Sussex (nobleman's son).'

The same heady atmosphere of *jeunesse dorée* settled over the venerable institutions entrusted with the higher education of these scions of our nobler houses. When it was decided that the eldest son of the Mikado of Japan should pursue his studies at Oxford, his name was entered for Magdalen and an official from the Japanese Embassy duly called on the then President, who had the justified reputation of being a fearful snob, to make the necessary arrangements for the Crown Prince's arrival. The President, a stickler for protocol, enquired how his new undergraduate should be addressed.

'At home it is customary to refer to him as the Son of God,' the diplomat told him guardedly.

'That will present no problem,' replied the President, 'we are used to receiving the sons of distinguished men at Magdalen.'

Dr Blakiston, President of Trinity College, Oxford, for over thirty years until just before the Second World War, held a similar esteem for his undergraduates of breeding. Complaining to the Dean about a noisy party held on a staircase near his Lodgings, he was a little perturbed to learn that the row had come from the rooms occupied by the elder Bathurst, who had been celebrating the end of training with his fellow-members of the college first Eight. The Bathursts have a long and distinguished association with Trinity and Blakiston was anxious to know what the crew had been up to. What had they been singing?

'The usual things,' the Dean told him, 'including marching songs common to their generation, some of them rather bawdy.'

'That,' replied the President, 'must have been most distasteful to Bathurst.'

Dr Jenkyns, sometime Master of Trinity's neighbour, Balliol, set his own store by rank and status. He stumbled on the pavement in the Broad outside the college and fell to the ground where two undergraduates hurried to his aid. As they offered their assistance he saw a MA walking towards him and cried, 'Stop, I see a Master of Arts coming down the street,' and dismissed the two lesser mortals with thanks, after the MA had helped him to his feet.

During the First World War Heathcote William Garrod, who taught Classics at Merton for most of his life and was the University Professor of Poetry for five years in the 1920s, was walking down a London street when a young lady handed him a white feather with the withering comment, 'I am surprised you are not fighting to defend civilization.'

'Madam,' replied Garrod, who was still in his thirties, 'I am the civilization they are fighting to defend.'

He died in 1960, one of the last of the old order, epitomized in their attitude to the demands of modern, time-efficient dictates from the Department of Education and Science by Professor Dawkins, at one time

Bywater and Sotheby Professor of Byzantine and Modern Greek Language and Literature at Oxford. Dawkins was asked once to give an account of how he spent his working time. 'I give an annual lecture,' he answered his inquisitor, 'but not every year, mark you.'

Nowadays attitudes like this are less easy to sustain, when Neville Lytton's ethic of 'Le style' doesn't cut much ice in the world at large.

Lord Wolfenden, formerly Vice-Chancellor of Reading University and later Director of the British Museum, knew about this. During his term as chairman of the University Grants Committee, he and his colleagues on the UGC were visiting northern universities and took a mini-bus from Leeds for their trip to the University of Hull. It was a very warm afternoon and en route the chairman suggested a break for a refreshing cup of tea; the committee agreed unanimously. So Lord Wolfenden asked the driver to pull into a roadside café. He was the first out and was striding towards the door in his shirt sleeves when it burst open to reveal the irate proprietor pointing to a sign in the forecourt, which none in the party had noticed, and yelling at his lordship, 'It says "No Coach Parties" – can't any of you lot read?'

Granted that this aura of exclusivity has been fostered for so many generations, the haughty attitudes of many undergraduates is understandable – if not condonable.

Sir Basil Blackwell used to tell of the occasion during his own student days at Oxford when a couple of undergraduates passed him on the street returning from a formal dinner, dressed up to the nines and several over the eight.

'The conversation was rather precious wasn't it?' he

heard one remark to the other.

'Yes,' said his friend, 'but I fancy I kept my end up.'

'Oh, most certainly; but if you don't mind me mentioning it, Botticelli isn't a wine.'

'Isn't it?'

'My dear chap, it's a cheese.'

This *hauteur* extends, or used to extend at any rate, to pinching policemen's helmets on Boat Race Night and other run-ins with the law. There was a Downing man who appeared before magistrates in Cambridge, charged with hanging on to the back of a lorry while riding a bicycle through the city. Asked for his defence he told the court, 'I had just taken part in a strenuous game of golf which had left me in a state of inertia, and my frantic effort at locomotion while riding into a strong headwind had sapped my last drop of energy. I felt these extenuating circumstances constitute some justification for an act which I readily agree in normal circumstances would be the acme of supreme indiscretion.'

'Very revealing,' remarked the magistrate. 'Ten shillings.'

Once in a while undergraduates do emerge who fully merit the aura of veneration that others try to cultivate for lesser merit. Such a young man was Charles Burgess Fry, an Oxford and college contemporary of Sir John Simon and F.E. Smith, with whom he formed a glittering triumvirate in the last decade of the nineteenth century.

Fry went up to Wadham with three pounds in his pocket, an eighty pound scholarship and no allowance from home. He took a first in Mods, became Senior Scholar in his college, captained the university football and cricket elevens and was President of the Athletic

Club (in which capacity he broke the world long-jump record – reputedly putting aside the cigar he was smoking before embarking on his historic leap).

He wasn't alone in his apparent effortlessness. At one time there was a modern-languages master at Edinburgh Academy, who was liked and respected by both staff and boys for his scholarship, his good natured attitude to school life and his absent-mindedness. At Oxford he had won an athletics Blue for throwing the javelin, although his principal recreation was the study of wild flowers. Apparently he had gone up to university with the assumption that games, or athletics at least, were compulsory, as they had been at school. He won his Blue before this misunderstanding had been corrected.

Maybe it's partly this abiding influence of school that bonds the upper classes within that other great circle of status – the old school tie.

This has been drawn on for guidance and assistance throughout a man's life. Before sentence was passed on a defendant appearing before a judge at Winchester, charged with burglary, the man in the dock pleaded, 'My old school has a very honoured name, sir. If you send me to prison I shall be the first Old Boy who has ever had such an indignity.'

In business it happened that many of the wide-boys of secondary banking went under after receiving rather risky loans in the boom years of the early 1970s often from fairly conservative banks, the merchant bank Lazard Frères & Co succeeded in emerging unscathed from similar bad debts. Lord Poole, the chairman of Lazards at the time, was asked by Lord Cowdray, chairman of the family business that owned the bank, how he had avoided entering into such potentially disastrous loans. 'Quite simple,' replied Lord Poole, 'I only lent money to people who had been to Eton.'

And in politics – when Stanley Baldwin was called to form a government, one of his first thoughts was 'that it should be a government of which Harrow should not be ashamed.' He set out to have six Harrovians holding cabinet posts and managed to achieve this by appointing himself Chancellor of the Exchequer.

The old rivalry between Eton and Harrow could sometimes be set aside for the demands of party loyalty. One fourth of June in the late 1930s the Conservative Government included in their whip the reminder that upwards of a hundred of their members were likely to be deserting the government benches for the day to attend their annual celebrations back at Eton. Non-Etonians were earnestly requested to fill the breach, none more so than former pupils of Harrow, whose motto, 'Stet fortuna domus', the whips felt certain would stand between them and defeat in a division. The fact that the Government Chief Whip was an old Harrovian no doubt added weight to the cause.

Only a few years later the same camaraderie helped avoid defeat from the common foe. As one newspaper reported, 'Sir Oliver Leese's appointment to command the Eighth Army makes our Mediterranean war an Eton and Harrow affair.' (Presumably because we were fighting on a larger area than Waterloo, the playing fields of Harrow had to be called on to join those below Windsor Castle in defeating a foreign tyrant.)

In peacetime, though, old enmities returned, as this personal advertisement in *The Times* one summer recorded:

Eton v. Harrow – Will numerous Harrovians who in attempting to divest a very old Etonian of his trousers deprived him of two treasured Five Shilling Pieces and gold safety pin, please return one or all to the Army and Navy Club?

Old boys of other distinguished institutions have occasionally established monopolies rivalling those of these two prominent schools. Half a century ago a former student of Trinity College, Oxford, wrote to the editor of the same newspaper:

By the lamented death of the Dean of Westminster a remarkable coincidence and (to an old Trinity man) a proud one, is broken through. Hitherto on his way north, he could have breakfasted with the Dean of Westminster, lunched with the Dean of Peterborough, had tea with the Dean of York, and dined with the Dean of Durham – all members of his college.

It's this sort of comfortable cabal that makes the public school legacy the envy of aspiration of anyone with eyes set on the higher things in public and social life. Perhaps that's why there's such a demand for old school ties, genuine and bogus.

At one time the market was flooded with unofficial Old Rugbeian ties with the stripes running in the wrong direction. These were cheaper than the official ties endorsed by the committee, because the direction of the stripe allowed more ties to be cut from a given piece of cloth. Members were urged 'to remain faithful to the official variety'.

Appearances may be deceptive, however, and the

unwary can frequently mistake a gentleman by relying too greatly on what they see on the surface. A young man, not long down from Winchester, was drinking in a hotel bar with an older and altogether more shabby man wearing an Old Wykehamist tie as frayed and battered as its owner. After eyeing him suspiciously for a while, the young man finished his drink and went across to the other to ask rather coolly, 'Excuse me. Why are you wearing an Old Wykehamist tie?'

'Because I can't afford a new one,' answered the older man, resuming his drink.

That's where breeding shows.

MANNERS
MAKYTH
MAN

EDUCATION IS ONLY ONE PART OF THE COMPLEX PROCESS of breeding those who will rise into the upper levels of the social swim. The acquisition of manners and the code of conduct that's summed up by 'correct form' plays an almost more important part in setting those who have a touch of class apart from those who manifestly haven't.

This indoctrination can begin nauseatingly early in some households. A thoroughly self-important six-year-old, leaving a friend's birthday party, said goodbye to his hostess at the front door with a fulsome, 'Thank you very much for inviting me. It's the very nicest party I've been to in all my life.'

'Oh, don't say that!' replied his friend's mother.

'But I *do* say that. I always say that,' he assured her.

For any youngsters less endowed with self-esteem the National Association of Girls' Clubs and Mixed Clubs once drew up a list of do's and don'ts to help their members get on in society. When taking leave of your hosts, for instance, these two bodies cautioned their members to thank their host and hostess as if they meant it; after staying the night, a 'thank you' letter should be sent.

Boys going out to meals were advised to enter the room punctually with clean shoes and without coat and hat. At parties boys had two points to watch out for: taking their share in the conversation and offering seats to others. (Taken too literally this conjures up very unsettling visions of eager youths constantly jumping up from their seats and breaking into what you're saying.)

Among so-called 'Town Manners' are tips like: don't throw cigarette ends on carpets; don't step dreamily out in front of traffic; don't grumble if an old, slow person is in front of you in a queue at a railway ticket office; don't make a noise outside hospitals.

(Personally, I think the most valuable piece of social advice I was ever given was 'Only serve red wine with a red carpet.')

There are a number of telling prohibitions categorized as 'Walking Manners', which range from helping old people and young children to cross roads, to warnings about not dashing out from behind stationary cars or stepping suddenly off kerbs. (This emphasis on methods of self-destruction suggests some curious tendencies among members of the Girls' and Mixed Clubs.)

The underlying message in all these interdictions and gentle hints is that the club members clearly needed to be taught them, if they were to blend with non-members who obviously knew them all already.

One wonders, however, just how many attentive nannies would have thought to pass on the timely warning to future train passengers offered by a correspondent to *Picture Post,* who wrote:

People who find it necessary to vomit whilst in a railway carriage should discreetly use their hats; this would come naturally to anyone properly brought up.

Which reminds one of that awful joke that still seems to appear in every batch of Christmas crackers:

Man (on seeing revolting specimen of modern youth), 'You say he was brought up at Eton? It looks to me as though he was eaten and then brought up.'

Of course the truly well bred never allow themselves to get into the state when they need to vomit – in public at any rate. Judith Listowel, the author of the *Manual of Modern Manners,* is uncompromising on the subject, telling her readers never to spit out anything. If you happen to burn your tongue on an unexpectedly hot mouthful, her advice is to eat some of the soft part of your bread roll 'and be more careful next time'.

Courtesy, she goes on to say, forbids the well bred to mention the presence of foreign bodies in their food, and by way of illustration she relates the case of her grandfather who, seated next to his hostess at a large dinner party, noticed a slug tucking into the lettuce he was about to consume. With perfect equanimity he delicately covered the creature with a fold of salad, closed his eyes and swallowed it. To drive the moral of the story home, it always concluded with the line, 'And your grandfather was not sick until dinner was over . . .'

Even the innocent process of enjoying the contents of a bowl of fruit contains pitfalls for the unwary. The *Daily Mirror* once printed the anxious enquiry:

Will you please tell me the correct way to eat grapes?
I have always eaten grapes by picking the fruit from the stem, conveying them to my mouth with my fingers, and removing pips by ejecting them into the hollow of my hands.

Passing the time of day wasn't always as straightforward as you might imagine: 'Is it correct for a lady visitor arriving for tea to ignore the maid who admits her, or to say good afternoon?' asked another anxious correspondent, adding, 'Also, should the maid say good afternoon if the lady ignores her?'

'You're dreadfully untidy again, Mary! I don't know what the baker will think of you when he comes.'
'The baker don't matter, 'm. The milkman's bin!'

These may seem trivial details, but it's only through carefully honed points of etiquette that the refined is picked out from the coarse in the tightly woven fabric of social distinction.

An example of what changes in this can portend is given in the case of an elderly and much respected City businessman who for years and years was a regular diner at a particular London restaurant. He was always served by the same waiter, whom he had grown into the habit of asking, 'How are you today?' For his part the waiter customarily replied, 'Good of you to ask, sir.'

'Then one day,' the diner explained, 'he suddenly started telling me how he was and I realized that a whole way of life had changed. The formality had been spoiled, and of course it was an awful bore because one didn't really want to know.'

It's through sticking to formulae like this that the classes manage to maintain a respectable distance between each other. Sweep them aside and all manner of misunderstandings can arise. 'Have I joined the middle class?' asked a reader of the *Sunday Graphic*. 'I find myself calling my doctor and my solicitor by their Christian names – and that I'm told is a criterion of middle-class establishment.'

There are things which you might do in one social milieu that you'd never consider in another – like keeping tabs on your possessions at a dance, as a reveller who lost her wrap at a ball found to her cost. 'Of course I didn't check to see if my stole was still there,' the lady in question told police called to the scene. 'At an ordinary dance or a village hop I would – but, after all, this was a hunt ball.'

How you behave inside your own front door is

another indicator of class. Dealing with a case of battery brought before him at Sheffield Assizes, Mr Justice Lawton commented, 'A bit of wife-thumping on a Saturday night may not amount to cruelty in some parts of England, but a bit of thumping in Cheltenham may be cruelty. The social background counts.'

That certainly goes for some towns and cities. An advertisement in *Homefinder* dwelt on the delights of Bath, which it described as 'one of the most beautiful cities in the Kingdom', adding as a further incentive, 'A large proportion of the inhabitants are of the distinctly residential class.'

In Eastbourne, members of the Eastbourne Comrades FC attending their annual meeting a long while back, heard an appeal from the management committee that they should drop the word 'Comrades' from their name: this was said to savour of Communism.

While residents in Cuckoo Hill Road, Pinner, complained to the local council when one of their number took to keeping a lion as a pet. What's interesting is that their complaint wasn't based on the danger the animal might pose to passers-by – they felt its presence 'lowered the tone of the area'.

If the pets you keep say something about your social status, so does the way they fit into your life, by all accounts. At one time dogs used to be charged for their train travel according to distance; no extra charge was levied if they went first class. This led to some interesting revelations to British Rail staff, one of whom commented, 'Mongrel dogs often travel first class and pedigree dogs usually travel third. I think it may have something to do with the wages situation.'

On the same subject, the brochure for a hotel in south Devon advised its guests that their dogs would

'That's Marcus in his prime — proud, arrogant and top of the heap, yet tenderness itself with his loved ones. I forget who the man is.'

be charged 'one shilling or one and sixpence per day according to size and social standing'. A little flattery can work wonders when you're after someone's money.

A little flannel is also useful. A court hearing a case of housebreaking in Blackpool was told by the prosecution that the two defendants had lived double lives for nine weeks, during which time they had been making a tidy penny from breaking and entering while maintaining an outward veneer of respectability. As counsel for one of them suggested to the judge, in mitigation, both men had suffered considerably. His own client, he explained, was a member of a golf club with a handicap of six, and as a consequence of the court case was now not only financially ruined, but socially disgraced as well.

Invariably those born to high positions have an easy superiority which elevates them effortlessly above the common herd. Edward VII was said to be such a man. During his long spell as Prince of Wales he impressed an American guest at a reception they attended by his easy-going manner. 'You know, he treated me as an equal,' remarked the American afterwards, more than favourably disposed towards the idea of royalty.

'Yes,' replied the English courtier to whom he made the remark, 'His Royal Highness is always ready to forget his rank – as long as everyone else remembers it.'

Of course, the Prince of Wales was no mean host himself. Guests at Sandringham weekend parties would be weighed on their arrival and departure. Any who failed to put on a pound or two had to answer to His Royal Highness himself.

Guests who were unable to accept his hospitality had their own ways of conveying their apologies. One of his closest friends, Lord Charles Beresford, once declined an invitation to dine with him with a telegram that read, 'VERY SORRY CAN'T COME LIE FOLLOWS IN POST' – which takes the limits of social candour to their extreme and is something that no one but a very close friend would dare to do, especially to the Prince of Wales.

The maid who was but human.

Beau Brummell discovered this to his cost after his brush with a previous incumbent of that title. Following their close friendship, the two quarrelled

violently leading to a rift which first came to public
attention at a reception that Brummell gave with his
friend Alvaney. When the Prince's arrival was
announced, the hosts and two other gentlemen took
up positions by the door holding lighted candles, to
receive their royal guest. When he entered the
gathering the Prince spoke very civilly to the two men
on his right and then turned to the man standing
beside Brummell and also uttered a few polite words to
him. In Brummell's own case, though, the Prince of
Wales looked right through him and without a flicker
of recognition walked on past into the room. Just as he
was about to greet the other guests, Brummell asked
his fellow host in a loud voice, 'Alvaney, who's your fat
friend?' That cost him his position at court and his
place in society.

The present Prince of Wales is altogether more
adept, even in the trickiest of situations. Meeting the
beauteous Súsan Hampshire wearing a very low-cut
gown at a theatrical gathering, he reportedly greeted
her without a trace of confusion, saying, 'Father told
me that if I ever met a lady in a dress like yours, I must
look her straight in the eyes.'

His father has his own brand of chivalry. Stopping
to talk to a couple of very elderly ladies on a visit to an
old people's home, the Duke of Edinburgh was told by
one of them, 'I'm a hundred and four and my friend
here is a hundred and one.'

'I don't believe a word of it,' said the Duke, with a
mischievous twinkle in his eye. 'Ladies always take ten
years off their age.'

Overbearing pomposity has often been mistaken by
the ill-bred for natural supremacy. The story is told of
a young subaltern freshly arrived from England who

joined the overseas unit to which he had been
seconded just in time for lunch. By way of making
conversation the officer across the table from him
asked, 'You're in the Norfolk Regiment, aren't you?'

'Yes,' replied the new arrival, with an air of scarcely
shrouded disdain, 'the Royal Norfolk Regiment.'

The embarrassed pause that greeted this was
eventually broken by a third officer asking pointedly,
'Excuse me, would you mind passing the Royal
Worcestershire Sauce?'

At my club, the Garrick, the cardinal sin is to
behave like a bore in any of his myriad forms. The
dramatist Freddy Lonsdale, who personified the
perfect behaviour expected of the club's members,
once found himself accosted by a stranger, who asked
bluntly, 'I say, aren't you Freddy Lonsdale?'

A swift survey was enough to satisfy Freddy as to
the man's possibilities. 'No, not tonight,' he told him.

During the last years of his very long life I took that
splendid old character actor, Walter Fitzgerald, to dine
at the Garrick. He had suffered a grievous car accident
and was now blind and very lame. A lady, a guest of
one of the members, spied Walter sitting under the
stairs with his white stick. She bounded over to him to
ask, 'Excuse me, are you Leslie Banks?'

'No,' said Walter. 'No, he's been dead much longer
than I have.'

Sir Herbert Beerbohm Tree suffered from a similar
oaf at the Garrick during his membership. This man
coupled acute snobbery with unutterable tediousness
and, telling Tree once, 'When I joined, all the members
were gentlemen,' he laid himself wide open for the
rejoinder, 'I wonder why they left.'

(Of course, this can't always have been true. When

'I'm afraid he's dead sir, but if I may be permitted: the Irishman pulls the rabbit out of his hat, and the vicar then says to the Jesuit priest . . .'

the Garrick was first founded some 150 years ago, the proposal was to establish a club where 'actors could meet gentlemen'. The supposition being that actors weren't gentlemen.)

The first Duke of Wellington was another who was punctilious in observing correct behaviour himself and exploring the absence of it in others. Climbing into his carriage one morning outside Apsley House, he was accosted by a complete stranger who shouted out with undue familiarity, 'Mr Smith, I believe.'

'If you believe that,' said the Duke, 'you will believe anything.'

The boot was on the other foot when Theodore Hook, the early nineteenth-century wit with an impish sense of fun, approached an exceedingly over-dressed man walking down the Strand to ask him, 'Excuse me, sir, but are you anybody in particular?'

Politicians are frequently exposed to the tempta-
tions of self-aggrandizement – and its nemesis. William
Joynson-Hicks, British parliamentarian and Home
Secretary in the latter half of the 1920s, suffered in this
respect from his long-standing adversary, David Lloyd
George.

Plain William Hicks had married the heiress Grace
Joynson in 1895 and had marked the event by adding
her surname to his own. Lloyd George did not forget
this and when Joynson-Hicks tackled him during one
of his Budget speeches with the question, 'Would the
right honourable gentleman define what he means by
the term "unearned increment"?,' the chancellor
pondered for a moment before replying, 'Certainly;
unearned increment is the hyphen in the honourable
gentleman's name.'

True modesty is an infinitely powerful ally, especially in politics. When a small force of police raided the
Beefsteak Club one evening early this century, in one
of their periodic measures to stamp out illicit
gambling, they questioned everyone in the building,
including all those dining there. At one table sat three
men, who, asked to identify themselves, politely
complied. One claimed to be the Belgian envoy;
another said he was the Speaker of the House of
Commons.

'And I suppose that you are the Prime Minister of
England?' enquired one of the detectives of the third
man.

'Yes, as a matter of fact I am,' answered A.J. Balfour
demurely.

This reserve permeates the upper levels of society to
emerge in any number of situations. Sir David
Edgeworth, the geologist and explorer, who was one of

Shackleton's companions on his South Polar expedition of 1907–9, displayed the characteristics of the true gentleman even in the frozen wastes of Antarctica.

Edgeworth's assistant, Douglas Mawson, was working in his tent one day when he heard a voice calling indistinctly from outside, 'Mawson, are you very busy?'

Recognizing the voice as Edgeworth's, Mawson called back, 'Yes I am. What's the matter?'

'Are you really *very* busy?'

'Yes, I am,' he yelled back in exasperation. 'What is it you want?'

There was a brief silence, after which Edgeworth answered apologetically, 'Well, I'm down a crevasse, and I don't think I can hang on much longer.'

Sang froid – in adversity there's nothing to beat it, though not everyone was convinced. Somerset Maugham expressed his reservations about it by always travelling in foreign ships. Asked why he did this, his answer was, 'Because there's none of that nonsense about women and children first.'

Field Marshal Montgomery wouldn't have agreed. His own composure, tinged with a fine sense of the dramatic, served him well in civilian as in military life. During a debate in the House of Lords, he turned to the peer sitting next to him and said calmly, 'Would you excuse me, but I'm having a coronary thrombosis.' Unaided he left the chamber in perfect control of himself and went in search of a doctor, who duly confirmed that he had indeed suffered a heart attack.

Of course, this reserve can be taken too far. J.M. Barrie used to tell of the occasion when he was in the reading room of the Athenaeum one day and, reaching for a newspaper, accidentally collided with an elderly professor. With his usual courtesy, Barrie made his apologies, but the old boy gripped him warmly by the hand and said with much feeling, 'Sir, thank you for those few kind words. I have been a member of this club for thirty years and you are the first member who has ever spoken to me.'

It can also lead to awkwardness in other company. 'I am a shy, retiring chap', admitted a correspondent to the *Daily Sketch* who signed himself 'Wallflower, Manchester', 'and not a great success at parties. The girls all flock round a man I know who can waggle his ears. How is this done? Or can anyone suggest an equally successful party trick?'

There can be a certain isolation too, as this advertiser implied in his plaintive line in the *Yorkshire Evening Post,* 'Gent, quiet, reserved, would like to meet gent.' – and that more or less sums up the lot of the man of breeding when detached from his fellows. The ladies, you note, don't get a look in.

Public decorum is another matter, when the way in which you conduct yourself, even when you're out enjoying an evening on the town, betrays your origins almost as much as asking for a dash of lemon with your port.

Your environment is important; as one frequenter of West End nightspots noted before the war, 'Everything is always so nice and correct at the Berkley: one feels that the spirit of Britannia is watching over one's behaviour, also over the cabaret turns, which also reflect a rather guarded outlook' – Munich, after all, wasn't too far in the distance.

As any well-bred person will tell you, words spoken on public occasions should also betray a similar modesty; being brief and to the point. Lord Chief Justice Hewart had a well-developed formula for replying to public speeches. Receiving some kind of public honour, he said in reply, 'On occasions of this kind there are two speeches which I can make; one is short and one is long. The short one is "Thank you," the long one is "Thank you very much." Now that I have acquainted you with the content of both speeches I see no reason for making either.'

Brevity of this sort might be construed as bordering on the frontiers of rudeness, but the man of breeding would favour that to the censure of being thought prolix.

F.E. Smith was once the subject of a long fulsome introduction at a livery company dinner, which began with his host rising to his feet and saying, 'I now call upon F.E. Smith, who needs no introduction from me . . .' and ended after he had given an introduction that lasted the best part of fifteen tedious minutes, with the same words, 'So, I now call upon F.E. Smith for his address.'

'It's Grosvenor Square,' he retorted furiously, 'and I'm going there right now.'

A gentleman is expected to make his contribution to dinner conversation all the same. Those who don't are likely to suffer the fate of the dinner-guest whose neighbour received a pencilled note from their hostess, delivered by the butler. Unfortunately the lady to whom it was addressed couldn't read it without her glasses and asked the taciturn man beside her if he would oblige. 'It reads,' he began, 'be a dear and please try to liven up the man on your left. He's a terrible bore, but do talk to him.'

At the other end of the scale is the guest who never knows when to stop talking. One who had committed the cardinal sin of way outstaying his welcome, finally

AFTER-DINNER TOASTS

Maid   *The guests – curse 'em!*

rose to leave and said to his flagging hosts, 'Thank you for a lovely evening. I did enjoy myself and I hope I haven't kept you up too late.'

'No – not at all,' replied the husband. 'We'd be getting up soon anyway.'

How different was the satisfying formality of the nightly farewell offered by the announcer in the early days of broadcasting which prompted a listener to comment:

> It is one of my greatest joys to listen to the natural, pleasant tones of the manly voice speaking English in its best form to which I am accustomed from the BBC. When I hear the announcer's pleasant 'Good night', I invariably reply audibly, 'Good night, dear man!'

Lord Reith's concern for establishing acceptable standards for the new public service got the BBC off to a flying start in the public decorum stakes. Not every institution could rely on such firm foundations. The *British Medical Journal* half a century ago gave its own explanation for declining standards of behaviour between the managed and managing in public life – misuse of the drug benzedrine. Even in small doses this was observed to involve 'a dangerous degree of disrespectfulness to superior officers on telephones'.

The theatre has frequently been viewed with distrust by self-appointed guardians of public probity, who more often than not feared the breaking down of social barriers as a threat to their own standards of living.

The shock waves that Bernard Shaw sent through polite society when he gave Eliza her famous expletive in *Pygmalion* were still lapping into the backwaters of suburbia when the film version of the play appeared, causing one incensed cinema-goer to complain:

> I saw half of it when a beautiful young lady actress was caused to utter the vilest expression I have ever heard in a public meeting – 'Not bl--dy likely.' I was so disgusted I walked straight out. The film is a disgrace to civilization. I hope you'll do your best to get it taken off.

The Lord Chancellor used to do his bit to maintain decency on the stage – amateur as well as professional. The Whitley Bay and Monkseaton Amateur Lyric Society submitted their annual pantomime script to his department for its scrutiny, in a year in which they planned to stage *Dick Whittington.*

When the script was returned one of the characters, formerly named Van Dam, had had his name altered to Van Drat.

Even more serious was the attack on a forthcoming production of Goldsmith's comedy *She Stoops to Conquer* a bare three days before it opened with the Holmfirth Amateur Dramatic Society. This broadside was delivered by the pastor of the local Lydgate Chapel, who began his tirade by stating that far too many in the world at large believed in the moral of the play – that all is fair in love and war, and there was nothing in the slightest bit wrong about stooping to conquer. He continued, 'Against this kind of immoral reasoning I, as a minister of religion, wish to protest. It has eaten like a canker into all departments of life.'

Continuing in this vein, he said, 'We have to thank the bad ethics taught by such plays as *She Stoops to*

Conquer for nearly all the irregularities, for all the adulteration of foods, tricks of trade, sweated labour, slacking and faking by men, jerry building and hoodwinking which are deeply rooted in our commercial, industrial and political life.'

As a passing shot he dismissed Goldsmith's time-honoured classic, claiming that he'd only written it because he was short of money and that it had a weak plot and not a single decent character!

The Church can reflect milder forms of censorship that sometimes betray its social leanings. At one time the Church House meeting in Salisbury decided to discontinue displaying *Punch* in its reading room, on the grounds that it was 'rather Socialist'. Two alternative periodicals were discussed as substitutes: the *Illustrated London News* and the *Methodist Recorder*.

Talking about religion can get a gentleman into hot water if he isn't careful, which is why this subject and that of money are eschewed at dinner. Even casual exchanges to pass the time can lead to frightful pangs of conscience which, as Hamlet reminds us, 'doth make cowards of us all'. One such sufferer of a dark night of the soul felt obliged to confess publicly in a personal advertisement:

> Does lady travelling home one night with bottle of sherry and Apochryphal Bible remember long conversation with travelling companion who hereby confesses with shame to having advanced blasphemous theories and has now bitterly repented of them?

It's a deep-seated respect for the divine which underscores so much of the general understanding of 'correct form'.

NATURAL RELIGION

Bishop (reproving delinquent page)   *Wretched boy!*
Who is it that sees and hears all we do, and before whom
even I am but a crushed worm?
Page   *The missus, my lord!*

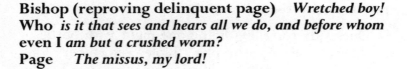

There was no more fitting example of this than Lord
Irwin's arrival in India to take up his appointment as
Viceroy. To the total confusion of the assorted VIPS
paraded to greet him with full imperial splendour, he
hurried off to church the moment his ship docked. It
was Good Friday and the allegiance uppermost in his

mind that morning was to his faith and not its defender snoozing peacefully in Buckingham Palace.

And there is no greater test of faith than the three-hour service on Good Friday. I remember a few years ago at my local church in Kensington we were about one and a half hours into the afternoon under the watchful eye of the visiting preacher, Cuthbert Bardsley, then Bishop of Coventry, when we launched into our fourth or fifth hymn. We were singing away quite contentedly when Cuthbert, who at the best of times resembled an Old Testament prophet, banged his hand on the pulpit rail. 'Stop ... stop ... stop,' he cried. 'Go back and start again. You are not thinking the words.'

This caused huge consternation amongst the extremely well-bred Kensington congregation. We duly went back to the first verse. This time the hymn was rendered with considerably more fervour.

The Good Lord is of course the acme of good breeding, though by some accounts the same isn't true of all His followers; at least not in the opinion of Jo Grimond. Asked whether he considered any of the saints to be gentlemen, he was forthright in his judgement on them. 'Exhibitionist, badly dressed, don't know how to behave and highly embarrassing,' was his summing up of this holy communion.

Even when the Spirit moves us, it would seem there's no excuse for failing to observe the tenets of correct behaviour.

MAINTAINING
STANDARDS

BEAU BRUMMELL, THAT ILL-STARRED ARBITER OF Regency taste, is said to have responded to the news that a young buck was so well dressed that he turned everyone's heads with the comment, 'In that case he was not well dressed.' Bertrand Russell would have agreed with him. Shortly before Eden became prime minister, the aging philosopher was asked his opinion of the forthcoming incumbent of No. 10. 'Not a gentleman,' Russell replied, 'dresses too well.'

In matters of first and often lasting impressions outward appearances invariably serve to distinguish the upper ten from everyone else.

This isn't a universally held opinion. There are those who regard one's outer appearance as secondary to more important issues – like national security. Early in 1940 General Sir Hubert Gough was bemoaning the ill-preparedness of the British Army to fight a modern war and harboured grave suspicions that the General Staff were too busy tackling the vital matter of officers wearing woollen scarves.

This aspect of military life had never been a great priority of his, and he confessed with some pride that a confidential report written on him as a young captain in the 16th Lancers in 1895 carried the severe censure, 'He takes no interest in dress.'

It has to be said that General Gough was rather out of step with the majority of his fellow officers and gentlemen in this respect. During the Boer War, the novelist John Buchan, serving as a young army officer, found himself carrying dispatches to Lord Haig, then Chief of Staff to General French. By coincidence, Buchan and Haig had been to the same Oxford college, as both knew. Unfortunately for Buchan, he overslept on the train and awoke with barely enough time to jump from his carriage at Colesberg, clad only in his pyjamas and greatcoat.

Thus attired he made his way to Haig's headquarters and was shown in to him. As he took the papers, Haig passed a brief glance over the young officer and merely commented, 'Brasenose never was a dressy college.'

I have every sympathy with the young Buchan. Some few years ago I was appearing in a musical in London's West End. The morning following one particular Saturday night performance I had arranged to record a television comedy programme in Manchester. I had to be in the studio at the crack of dawn and it was therefore essential that I caught the midnight train. As a consequence my planning was worthy of a military operation. During the second act I took a sleeping draught to assure instant sleep when I boarded the train.

Immediately the curtain fell I changed into pyjamas, dressing-gown and slippers. A hired car sped me to Euston where I hoped the sleeping carriage would be waiting.

When I arrived, however, I discovered to my horror that since my last visit they had decided to demolish the old station. Instead of the car being able to drive straight on to the platform, I was deposited some considerable distance away in the Euston Road.

I picked my way through the rubble, clad in my night attire and clutching my suitcase, and to those passing I must have resembled an old Arab carpet-

seller. Worse was to come, for as I reached the
platform the loudspeaker gave the news that the night
train would be an hour late leaving.

The sleeping draught was now rapidly taking effect.
I rallied sufficiently to fumble in my pockets for my
carriage ticket and handed it shakily to a passing porter
before curling up on a station bench and falling fast
asleep. I don't remember any more. But such must
have been the kindness of the porter that I woke up
the next morning safely tucked up in my bunk as the
train slowly pulled into Manchester Piccadilly.

In Court circles, of course, correct dress is a
prerequisite, and when the Duke of Kent married
Princess Marina in 1934 the Lord Chamberlain felt
beholden to direct 'that gentlemen invited to the
wedding who do not possess uniform or Court dress
should wear evening dress with trousers'.

Anyone who ventures to strike out on his own is
likely to get very short shrift. Such was the fate of Lord
Harris when he attempted a minor social breakthrough
in the Royal Enclosure at Ascot by appearing in a
bright tweed suit in place of the orthodox frock coat
and top hat. 'Mornin' Harris,' was Edward VII's chill
greeting. 'Goin' rattin'?'

Points of sartorial detail can be taken to even finer
degrees. Few gentlemen would be seen with the lower
button of their waistcoat buttoned. Fewer still would
allow themselves to wear a fountain pen (or worse still
a biro) in an outside pocket to a coat or jacket.

The Health Committee in Bristol once found itself
earnestly debating whether a soft hat or a bowler was
the more appropriate headgear for a sanitary inspector.

On the hunting field a revolution as dramatic as
Lord Harris's rocked the Cottesmore Hunt before the

war. This was instigated by women followers who had grown tired of the bowlers or toppers that were accepted headgear for them and unilaterally took to wearing the velvet caps that had formerly been the exclusive preserve of the huntsmen. The crisis came to a head when a prominent member of the committee threatened to close his land to the hunt unless the recalcitrant women returned to wearing what was right and proper.

The situation was every bit as bad in the Southdown Hunt in the early 1970s, which led the Master, Major Bruce Shand, to lament, 'It comes hard for a chap to have to say it but some of the people who go with these hounds these days are a shower. One doesn't like to wave a big stick, but we can't have people turning up as if they have been wearing the same pyjamas for a month.'

On the other hand a gentleman who takes care over his appearance, even in the saddle, can go to infinite pains to ensure that he is smartly turned out. One Savile Row tailor used to boast a client, a peer's son, who would always bring a couple of servants with him whenever he attended a fitting for a pair of breeches. If the servants were able to pull the breeches off his legs, he demanded an alteration.

Discipline in dress, some maintain, reflects discipline in life. *The Grocer's Handbook* carried the interesting observation, 'I believe in stiff collars on ethical and national grounds. They are a bulwark against lawlessness.'

Old standards die hard. When the Birmingham Press Club presented Enoch Powell with its tie, he admitted, as he struggled to substitute it for the one he was wearing, that until his private secretary had told him, he had had no idea that collar-attached shirts were on sale.

Trousers also have their part to play. Fifty years ago a shop in Regent's Street carried the advertisement:

> We modestly suggest that more can be done for democracy by wearing corduroys than all the efforts of the politicians put together. Try a pair, you will like them. It's a man's trouser!

Where you buy your clothes naturally counts for a good deal as well. When it was reported that Gieves had recorded less spectacular sales of shirts one Christmas than some of its larger competitors, a spokesman explained, 'We have heard of the bonanzas enjoyed by some of the big stores. Our customers are probably more susceptible to government policies – they tend to have their money in the City you know; whereas the Oxford Street type shopper keeps it in a jar on the mantelpiece.'

Ultimately, though, it's how and when you wear your wardrobe that matters when it comes to telling you apart from the man in the street. Cecil Rhodes was a stickler for correct dress and behaviour, though he never let this cloud his sense of good manners. Among the guests once invited to dine with him at his home in Kimberly was a young man who arrived by train and without time to change had to go directly to Rhodes's house in his travelling clothes. There he found the other guests dressed up to the nines and waited in acute discomfort for his host to appear.

After a considerable time Rhodes made his entrance wearing a battered old blue suit. Only later did his young guest learn that his host had been in full evening dress like everyone else and on the point of welcoming his guests when he heard about the young traveller's dilemma and immediately went back to his dressing-room to put on the tattiest suit he could find.

It's just a pity that more people aren't as sensitive to the feelings of others in circumstances like these. Magistrates in London were treated to a case in the mid-1970s involving a young patron of Pinkies, a restaurant in the metropolis, who appeared before them supported on a pair of crutches following an altercation with four of the restaurant's waiters. It appeared that they had been asked to evict the diner following his refusal to leave because he wasn't wearing a tie. 'Under normal circumstances I would have left without saying a word,' explained the defendant, 'but as it was a topless restaurant I thought they were going a bit far.'

The British Boxing Board of Control sought to introduce a touch of class into its contests when it issued a 'fashion-code' for fights banning braces for boxers' seconds. Anxious to dispel doubts that there was any 'personal significance' in the directive a spokesman said, 'We simply want to give our fights "tone".'

Sartorial guidance in more refined circles was handed out by the former Duke of Marlborough to two of his dinner-guests. The husband, a peer of the realm himself, mentioned casually during the course of the meal that he was thinking of having a velvet smoking-jacket made by his tailor. Hearing this, the Duke counselled sagely, 'My dear, nobody wears velvet after May.'

The following day the tailor received instructions to make the jacket, but in raw silk.

Maid   *There's a much better tone in this house now, m'm, than there used to be.*
Lady   **(indignantly)** *Indeed! I don't understand you Chalmers.*
Maid   *Oh, m'm, I mean downstairs, of course. Not upstairs.*

The guidelines of acceptability are no less exacting for the feminine wardrobe. For two hours a golf club committee in the south-east of England debated whether or not women players were to be allowed to wear slacks while playing a round of golf. In spite of the time devoted to the subject their eventual ruling was phrased with an unfortunate air of ambiguity: 'Trousers may be worn by women golfers on the course, but must be taken off on entering the clubhouse.'

It isn't only a social significance that's carried by a carefully selected wardrobe. As Alison Settle pointed out in the *Observer* shortly after the outbreak of the Second World War: 'One of the things we have learned from refugee friends escaping from France (via machine-gunned roads, ditches and holds of ships) is that a knitwear suit is the most desirable of possessions.'

A few months later it was a similar concern with the demands of *haute couture* which lent a common suffering to rich and poor alike, aptly summed up by the commentator who viewed the bombed-out shells of 'certain feminine emporiums' during a bus ride down Oxford Street and Regent Street and was moved to write, 'Nothing has brought home to women who "dress", more realistically than these gaunt ruins of autumn-sale rendez-vous the frightfulness of the *Blitzkrieg*.' War has always been a great leveller.

When that particular conflict had passed and the New Look promised better times to come, *Vogue* was in the vanguard of hailing the resurgence of the British fashion houses, leaner and grittier, by all accounts, after their six years of struggle. 'The London designers make clothes for real women,' stated the magazine; 'for women who live in the country, drive cars, go shopping, lunch out, sit on committees, drop in for drinks, go to Ascot, give parties, holiday abroad.' Clem Attlee would have been proud of them.

But to return to our starting point, that the well-bred are careful to shun ostentatious display, there's a telling anecdote from the early days of Mrs Thatcher's administration when she found to her dismay that she and the Queen were wearing the same dress when they met for one of the Prime Minister's weekly audiences. Anxious to avoid a repetition, Mrs Thatcher determined in the future to find out in

Mistress   *Can you explain how it is, Jane, that whenever I come into the kitchen I always find you reading?*
Jane   *I think it must be them rubber 'eels you wears, ma'am.*

advance how Her Majesty would be dressed. However, when one of her staff rang Buckingham Palace to arrange this, a member of the Royal Household explained that it wouldn't be necessary. 'You see,' he announced, 'the Queen never takes any notice of what her visitors are wearing.'

Queen Victoria, despite her reputation for unbending propriety, was perfectly capable of displaying the best of good manners when the occasion demanded. Dining in state during the visit of an eastern potentate the Queen noticed her guest of honour cheerfully sipping water from his finger-bowl. Without further ado and to spare her guest any embarrassment at this minor *faux pas,* the Queen took up her own finger-bowl and followed his example.

The knowledge of this story perhaps helped save me from a similar fate when I was honoured to be asked to luncheon recently in the same household. Needless to say, I, together with all the other guests, was decidedly nervous. Towards the end of the meal and before the arrival of the fruit, finger-bowls were duly placed somewhat forrard of each guest upon quite beautiful lace doilies. A distinguished sportsman sitting opposite me looked somewhat nonplussed and then very tentatively started to slide his bowl towards him, spoon at the ready. An eagle-eyed footman moved very slowly forward and gently slid a fruit plate between the guest and the approaching bowl of water. All was saved once again.

Table manners can be a minefield for the ill-informed; at times it seems as if they were deliberately designed to be so. But the food you eat, the crockery you use, the wines you serve, the hospitality you offer – each contributes a small portion of the picture of your social make-up.

The extent of your larder says a great deal about the attention you pay to the finer things in life. This delightful exchange hints at an opulence few could rise to but which the Rothschilds took effortlessly in their stride, especially at their country seat at Waddesdon. Asquith was staying there for a weekend during his premiership and at teatime the butler came to ask him, 'Tea, coffee, or a peach from the wall, sir?'

'Tea, please.'

'China, Indian or Ceylon, sir?'

'China, please.'

'Lemon, milk or cream, sir?'

'Milk, please.'

'Jersey, Hereford or Shorthorn, sir?'

At a slightly humbler level, but still carefully delineating one class of diner, or should one say gourmet, comes this comment from Katherine Whitehorn: 'I was eating moussaka in Bolton the other day which (though nice) was made of potato, and it suddenly made me realize just how little you can take aubergines for granted out of town.'

On the other side of the coin lies the case of striking stevedores in London's Victoria Dock who flatly refused an appeal to unload a shipment of forty-one tons of melons that were ripening in the hold with alarming haste. They gave as their reason the fact that in their opinion the melon was not a working man's fruit.

What about vegetables? They betray tell-tale clues of their own, it would appear. Forty years ago it was reckoned that if you took your lunch or dinner with a salad you were probably 'upper class'. Eating raw tomatoes and carrots was considered by this particular observer to be 'a mark of high social class. But serve potatoes only without vegetables, and your lower class origins are showing.'

When I first joined the theatre in 1952 we still had food rationing, and luxury items were in scarce supply. I took digs with a theatrical landlady in Bolton. One day whilst I was at the Hippodrome rehearsing for the following week's production, my mother arrived, worried about my welfare. With my landlady she left for my supper on my return from the theatre a fillet steak and a bunch of asparagus the like of which my landlady had not seen before. When I got home that evening I was greeted by the cheery old soul saying, 'Hallo, Mr Nimmo, yer mam came this afternoon. I've cooked the steak and I've put the bluebells in water.'

Food follows fashion, there's no denying, and sometimes it's frightfully *avant-garde* to tuck into something you wouldn't have given house room a few months earlier — and I don't just mean bran and wholefood confections. *Woman's Mirror* picked up one of these tides of culinary enthusiasm when it informed its readers:

> There is a tremendous vogue among really smart people for frightfully good, plain cooking. Steak and kidney pudding, apple tart, even cottage pie. In Belgravia and Chelsea, of course. Not in the suburbs where these things tend to be eaten every day.

For those who care about food and what is generally termed *haute cuisine,* there can be few disappointments in life greater than that described by Anthony Powell when he wrote, 'Dinner at the Hunterscombes possessed only two dramatic features — the wine was a farce and the food was a tragedy.'

Beau Brummell would have shared his scorn; at least as far as the wine was concerned. His palate matched his wardrobe and his diet, and anything that failed to rise to his exacting standards received no quarter. He was dining once at a house in Hampshire where the champagne served harboured no illusions of being anything but a very inferior cru. Waiting for a break in the conversation, Brummell called loudly to the wine waiter, 'John, give me some more of that cider, will you?'

A connoisseur with a taste for fine wines every bit as refined as Beau Brummell's used to boast that water had never passed his lips. When a young colleague asked innocently, 'But, sir, surely you clean your teeth?' he had a ready answer. 'Yes, of course, for my teeth I use a light Moselle.'

A fellow bon viveur, who also viewed blind Dom Perignon's sparkling discovery as a supreme gift to mankind, was moved to comment, 'Quite apart from wanting champagne as a party or aperitif drink, there can be few people who, during the often dreary strenuousness of November, don't actually need it as the world's supreme tonic.'

The only trouble with having a taste for fine wines is that you can attract the unwelcome attention of self-styled connoisseurs who like to pit their palates against yours.

A relatively young peer of the realm, who had already established a respectable reputation for his excellent cellar, gave a dinner party after a day's hunting to a large group of associates that included many guests far older than he. When the port was served he noticed one of the company, also renowned for his knowledge of wines, nosing and examining the colour of his drink with an air of considerable doubt. His young host asked if anything was the matter, to which the older man answered that he thought the port was corked.

At this cue the others ceased sipping their glasses and confirmed to a man that indeed the port was corked.

Their host summoned his butler and asked him to fetch the other decanter.

This was duly brought, along with fresh glasses, and was passed round. One sip was enough to confirm that this was definitely superior. The young master of the house smiled reassuringly and asked his butler, 'Which bottle of port is this?'

'It's the other half of the magnum, my lord,' he replied.

Another of the problems that may arise from a general dissemination of good taste is that it spreads to those without the financial means to sustain their

'I'm sorry, m'lady, but I'm afraid his grace is away on safari — right down the other end of the drive.'

newly acquired sensibilities – that's an argument perpetrated by the well-to-do, at any rate.

In the time when the guinea was still a means of paying people other than on the racecourse, the butler of a Tory MP who earned seven guineas a week bemoaned the difficulties he faced in maintaining himself in the style to which he had become accustomed. 'I'm having a terrible struggle to keep up my wife's maintenance payments and maintain my own high standard of living,' he said. 'I have a twelve-shilling hair-cut once a fortnight, and I use a very expensive toilet water – the same in fact as Mr Anthony Armstrong-Jones. It costs 14s 6d for a tiny bottle.'

Not everyone is generously minded about their annual breaks. 'Are you tired of meeting the workers on holiday?' asked an advertisement in *The Economist*. 'Don't let them spoil it for you next year. Travel to exclusive places by scheduled jet at realistic prices.'

Perhaps there were other reasons for getting away from familiar shores. As air travel started to become more commonplace and seat prices fell it opened the doors to what one travel writer called, 'people of limited means', allowing them, 'to take modest holidays abroad now that they can be sure that friends and acquaintances will not be staying, to their embarrassment, in more exclusive hotels in the same resort.'

Naturally, different people have different holiday expectations though most have a pretty clear idea of what does or doesn't appeal to us – like the 'camper' who pulled out of a holiday camp after just a day's stay, taking his wife and three children with him, because there was no knock-knees or beauty competitions on Sunday.

The good people of Frinton, the East coast's most exclusive holiday resort, weren't sure that the idea of a fish and chip shop wholly appealed to them, and the town council had to go into secret session to debate the matter when the planning application for the first chippie in Frinton was submitted.

This preoccupation with your immediate environment is another crucial element in keeping up appearances and one that can make us fiercely protective.

Residents in a road in Sale succeeded in winning rate reductions from the local council when a Methodist church, Sunday school and community hall were built nearby, thus in their opinion lowering the tone of the area.

Down in London an even finer social distinction was drawn in Cornwall Terrace, overlooking Regent's Park, when squatters won their battle against dossers who had moved in, and apparently lowered 'the tone of their neighbourhood'.

But for anyone really anxious about saving face there can't be many hang-ups greater than that of the reader of *Reynold's News*, who wrote, 'Is any other reader afraid of the dustmen? When they call I always hide, just in case they say anything about the type of rubbish I put in the bin.'

When keeping up appearances reaches these dimensions you can't help wondering if it isn't better to let go and slip into genteel poverty. After all, as the author of *Passionate Kensington* noted, 'the world needs contrast and slums supply it'.

THE DAILY ROUND, THE COMMON TOIL

TRADITIONALLY THE WELL-TO-DO HAVE FREQUENTLY HAD a rather ambivalent attitude towards work, and those who undertake it. Before the arrival of the Yuppies and the near apotheosis of the City with its Mammon-like seductions, the work ethic was one greatly admired by those who didn't have to work, while anyone who was actually obliged to immerse themselves in the daily round and common toil was kept at a respectable distance.

When a former captain in the Indian Army suffered the indignity of being told by a magistrate that he should pull himself together in civvy street and go down a coal mine, the officer was none too thrilled at the idea. Outside the court he displayed his perfectly manicured hands to friends and relatives, telling them with pride, 'These hands never did a hard day's work in their lives. These are the hands of a gentleman.'

As revealing a comment came from the obituary in a local paper of an East Anglian landowner who had recently passed away. In recalling his occupation it was stated that he had 'worked on a farm for most of his life'. The following week a correction was printed to the effect that the sentence should have read that he 'had been a farmer most of his life.'

On the other hand, a man in his position is usually wary of blowing his trumpet too loudly. For example, I like the story of another prosperous wheat baron holidaying with his family in an expensive chalet near Davos. They became friendly with an equally well-off

German family and, in the course of getting to know each other, the Englishman said that he farmed for a living.

'You are a big owner of land?' asked the German father.

The Englishman said he wasn't; he was simply a farmer.

This didn't satisfy his German friend who said in some bewilderment, 'But you are not a peasant', and remained puzzled for a moment or two until the penny dropped: 'Oh, you are a gentleman farmer.'

Blushing ever so slightly, the Englishman corrected him firmly: 'Just a farmer.'

Those with independent means, however, can be quick to point out the burden these impose. One financial journalist, siding with anyone 'who holds enough investments to produce an income of £2,000', gave a rundown of the work involved in managing them. The investor has to keep a constant check on his holdings, he explained, selling some and buying others as the market dictates. To do this efficiently he may even have to sacrifice a room or two in his home to accommodate his financial affairs. 'Nevertheless', he concluded indignantly, 'he gets no relief at all for this.'

Taxation has always been a bugbear, in extreme cases forcing the seriously rich into offshore tax havens. Sir Bernard Docker spoke for many when he commented, 'We are tired of working for nothing – or varying degrees of nothing.' And in 1967 he and Lady Docker upped sticks and moved across the waters to Jersey. 'There are lots of reasons for the move,' he explained. 'Income tax is only four shillings in the pound and there are no death duties.'

The idyll was short-lived for all his optimism, and

'Heavens no. I'm only the caretaker.'

less than two years after their arrival the Dockers were on the move again, leaving behind their fellow refugees from the Revenue, who in Lady Docker's view were 'the most frightfully boring, dreadful people that have ever been born'.

When circumstances do force a man of good education and affluent background to support himself, against his own inclination, the results are sometimes patchy. If the old-boy network doesn't do the trick, there's always the slightly wider market, appealed to by personal advertisements like this: 'Active Englishman (50), with correct outlook, seeks work.'

Younger aspirants not blessed with a surfeit of grey matter may prefer trying their hands at some real work, particularly as the wages for skilled labourers compare very favourably with the sort of mundane desk jobs that they might otherwise end up with. Success can't be guaranteed and potential employers are rightly cautious of the public school boy who fancies toning up his muscles and acquiring a suntan with a few weeks on a building site before disappearing to St Tropez for the rest of the summer to crew on a friend's yacht.

A typical example was the young fellow killing time between leaving Charterhouse and going to Bristol University who presented himself to a foreman of his uncle's building firm with ideas of being taken on as a bricklayer. This idea was dismissed out of hand. 'Hod-carrier?' pondered the foreman. 'No ... I don't think so. I'll tell you what. Why don't we start you as an architect and let you work your way up?'

And that's the major drawback with the real world of work in the eyes of many who consider themselves to be above the madding crowd – it's a great leveller which shows scant regard for social or intellectual status.

Among the unfortunate casualties of this harsh reality was a hospital chaplain whose place in the pecking order was determined solely by his income. As a result he started out with a bare two weeks' holiday a year and meals in the same canteen as the clerks. It took some time before one of the hospital's more enlightened administrators got wind of his plight and arranged for him to eat with the doctors in future, doubling his annual leave into the bargain.

When it comes to offering guidance to people lower down the social scale on how they should occupy themselves, the well-to-do have always felt on firmer ground. One suggestion made during the Depression to improve life for the unemployed was that everyone earning over £2,000 a year should adopt a man on the dole and 'help him preserve his sense of proportion by sending an occasional cheerful letter or an old book'.

For a while Neville Lytton sat as a JP, and during this time he presided over a case of poaching which in his opinion had an obvious solution that stood to benefit both the accused and society as a whole. The poacher was a lad in his teens who'd been caught by the village policeman with a pheasant stuffed into his jacket. This had apparently been shot through the eye with a catapult on a night when there was no moon. Neville Lytton was impressed and tried to persuade his fellow-magistrates that the young culprit should be let off, so that he could be sent to join the army as a King's marksman. Regrettably for Lytton, and even more for the lad, this wasn't a solution favoured by the rest of the bench.

This facility for organizing other people's lives has

been carefully nurtured by the ruling classes, and had one of its most striking personifications of sheer grandeur in the figure of Lord Curzon. Being made Viceroy of India at the age of only thirty-nine can have done little to curb his legendary air of privileged pre-eminence.

During his time at Balliol a fellow-undergraduate wrote of him:

> My name is George Nathaniel Curzon,
> I am a most superior person.
> My face is pink, my hair is sleek,
> I dine at Blenheim once a week.

These lines foreshadowed his career in public life with uncanny accuracy. (It was Curzon, interestingly, who reviewed a menu to be offered by his old college during a royal visit many years later and returned it with a note in the margin, 'No gentleman has soup at luncheon.' Little wonder Max Beerbohm referred to him as 'Britannia's butler'.)

His understanding of the world at large was limited. The celebrated story is told of the occasion when he decided to sample public transport for the first time and hailed a bus in Whitehall, telling the driver to take him to Carlton House Terrace (his London home); he was most surprised when the man adamantly refused.

On another occasion he was walking past a jeweller's shop in Bond Street when he paused, peering into the window, and asked the friend with him, 'What is that?' – indicating a small cylinder of silver.

'That's a napkin ring, Curzon,' the friend answered benignly.

'Really? What is it for?'

'Well, Curzon,' his friend began uncertainly, 'there are some households in which fresh linen cannot be provided at every meal. So, when they have finished eating, the diners roll up their napkins and place them in this ring, ready for their next meal. It saves unnecessary washing, you see.'

Curzon looked back at the napkin ring and said in pitying wonder, 'Can there be such poverty?'

Never did he let his public duty interfere with his life as a peer of the realm. Staying once at Kedleston, his principal country seat, he was summoned to the telephone to answer a call from his private secretary at the Foreign Office. Vansittart wanted to tell him urgently that news had just come through of the death of a particular foreign statesman. Curzon wasn't impressed. 'Do you realize, that to convey to me this trivial piece of information,' he answered, 'you have forced me to walk the length of a mansion not far removed from the dimensions of Windsor Castle?'

His disappointment when Stanley Baldwin was chosen to replace Bonar Law as Prime Minister was apparent to all. Not only was Baldwin from Harrow (Curzon had been to Eton); in his words Baldwin was 'Not even a public figure.'

For his part, Baldwin felt Curzon's chill, even though he continued to serve him as Foreign Secretary. 'I met Curzon in Downing Street,' he recalled, 'from whom I got the sort of greeting a corpse would give to an undertaker.'

Baldwin summed himself up as the quintessential English gentleman and a country gentleman at that. 'I speak not as the man in the street even,' he readily acknowledged, 'but as a man in a field-path, a much simpler person steeped in tradition and impervious to new ideas' – qualities that made him an ideal Conservative prime minister, of the old school.

And when the nation and empire were shaken to their foundations by Edward VIII's lamentable decision to marry the woman he loved, Baldwin's qualities were broadly appreciated. A.G. Macdonnell thought that it was because Baldwin was 'so completely an Englishman' that he was able to handle the crisis with such tact and composure. 'There is no coincidence,' he went on, 'in the fact that Mr Baldwin comes from Worcestershire, and Shakespeare from Warwickshire, counties that are the very core of England.'

Stanley Baldwin was also a shining example of good manners in practice. Hurrying down St James's on the way to the Commons one day he was spotted by a flag-seller who left her pitch and pushed after him through the crowds of Christmas shoppers to persuade him to buy a flag. Catching up with the Prime Minister, she touched his arm and offered him a flag. But Baldwin kept on walking.

The flag-seller returned to her corner and was delighted a couple of minutes later to see a familiar face struggling through the crowds towards her.

'Did you ask me to buy a flag just now?' asked Baldwin. 'I am so sorry; I didn't mean to be ungracious, but I was in the midst of composing a speech, and I was miles away.'

His common touch extended to his own employees.

One day a very embarrassed worker in the family business, only recently married, came to Baldwin to tell him that he'd broken the bridal bed.

Baldwin offered to have it mended free of charge at the company's foundry, but the poor man was terrified of the ribbing he'd get from his workmates. So that night the bed was brought secretly to the back door of Baldwin's house, where it was wheeled across the hall the next morning and out through the front door on its way to the works, just as if it had been the proprietor's own bed.

Winston Churchill once said of a Parliamentary candidate, 'He is asked to stand, he wants to sit, and he is expected to lie,' but Baldwin and politicians like him didn't always toe the line in the way that some of their longer established supporters in the aristocracy might have wished.

In 1931 Baldwin made a speech during a by-election and delivered his celebrated attack on the press barons: 'The proprietors of the national newspapers are aiming at power, and power without responsibility, the prerogative of the harlot throughout the ages.' Hearing this, the Duke of Devonshire, a firm supporter of. Conservative principles, commented, 'That's done it. He's lost us the tarts' vote now.'

His predecessors were no better pleased at times with their fellow-politicians. When Sir William Harcourt introduced his 1894 Budget, which included the revolutionary idea of death duties, the then Duke of Devonshire, who had turned down the premiership himself, was vigorous in his opposition to it.

At dinner one evening Lady Harcourt found herself seated next to her husband's principal adversary and remarked apologetically, 'Your Grace, I feel you would like to hang my husband.'

'No, madam,' replied the Duke, 'merely suspend him for a period.'

The aristocracy weren't the only people to have misgivings about the nation's leaders. A correspondent to the *Evening Standard* wrote: 'Gone, unfortunately, are the days when independent incomes assured us of a Parliament mirroring our feelings.'

Some time earlier the same paper had reported that a major effort to improve the intellectual ability of Conservative MPs had led to the Party Chief's 'move to make character and ability, rather than wealth, the qualifications for adopting candidates'.

Social criticisms of Socialist leaders took a different form. Chips Channon found Ramsay Macdonald a terrible snob, claiming that the only time he'd seen him smile was when he'd been talking to an elder son; although he did acknowledge that Macdonald was once pleasant to him the day after his last royal dinner party had been written up in the papers.

And moving nearer the present, Harold Macmillan's night of the long knives was viewed with distaste by at least one old Tory who thought it didn't seem 'quite the behaviour of a gentleman'.

Macmillan's successor, Sir Alec Douglas-Home, was chided by Harold Wilson, when he took over at Number 10, with the man of the people jibing at his hereditary position as the fourteenth Earl of Home. In reply the new premier refused to enter into a class wrangle and merely commented, 'As far as Fourteenth Earl is concerned, I suppose that Mr Wilson, when you think of it, is the fourteenth Mr Wilson.'

If his very early experiences were anything to go by, plain Alec Douglas-Home might have been chancing his luck when he renounced his peerage and fought the Kinross by-election. Mrs Florence Hill, who had acted as his under-nurse when he was only a year old, told reporters during the election, 'I had to see that Master Alec didn't talk to the servants and that he didn't leave our part of the house.'

Departing cook *You may be a viscountess but you ain't a lady.*

It says a lot for British democracy that both electors and their elected came through that schooling relatively unscathed.

The same confidence buttressed Nancy Astor, the first woman to take a seat in the House of Commons, when she took over from her husband as MP for Plymouth, after his elevation to the Upper House. To a heckler who taunted her with the question, 'Your husband's a millionaire, ain't he?' she struck back with the answer, 'I should certainly hope so, that's why I married him.'

In our own time there was the charming episode in the Palace of Westminster when the Lord Chancellor's procession was making its way down one of the long corridors along which a party of awed tourists were being guided. Behind them Lord Hailsham spotted his friend Neil Marten, in whose direction he raised his arm in a wave. 'Neil,' he called, and to a man (and woman) the party of visitors promptly knelt.

There's also a calming reassurance in the relaxed approach that those born to high office take to the great affairs of state – a touch of class if ever there was one. While the world was racing headlong towards the Second World War, there were still key figures in the British Government able to show that life was continuing unchanged in their world. As one commentator observed of the Prime Minister in the spring of 1939, 'But for the Albanian affair Mr Chamberlain would have landed his first salmon of the year.'

A year or two later the *Daily Mail* had reassured its readers that in spite of worrying reports from the Far East the situation in the region couldn't have been too bad, because only the night before its correspondent had bumped into Duff Cooper, still First Lord of the

Admiralty, at a cinema in Leicester Square.

Even after the Munich crisis in 1938 the then Foreign Secretary, Lord Halifax, was able to reply to a reporter who'd asked if he wasn't exhausted by all the late nights, 'Not exactly. But it spoils one's eye for the high birds.'

In 1948, the year when George Orwell was putting the finishing touches to *1984*, a radio station in Washington decided to invite a number of ambassadors serving in the city to say what they'd like for Christmas. Each was telephoned and his unedited reply was broadcast the following week in a special programme.

The French Ambassador hoped for peace throughout the world. His Russian counterpart wanted universal freedom from imperialism.

'Well, it's very kind of you to ask,' replied the diffident tones of Sir Oliver Franks, His Majesty's Ambassador to the United States. 'I'd like a small basket of crystallized fruit.'

Slightly more on the ball but displaying the same admirable politeness was Sir John Simon, who, as a fellow of All Souls, Oxford, was dining in the college one evening with many distinguished colleagues. Making up their number was one of the university's brilliant scholars who hoped too to be elected to a fellowship, and in time-honoured tradition was under close scrutiny as they dined.

This chap's family had a long association with India and once he'd moved the conversation on to the subject of the sub-continent, he was able to hold forth with confidence and conviction, impressing his hosts by his clarity of thought and force of argument.

Only Sir John Simon questioned one of the points

he made, in the mildest tones. Sensing the challenge, the would-be fellow, more trenchant than tactful, rounded on him and made it perfectly clear that he knew a good deal more of the subject than his questioner.

'I'm naturally extremely interested in your views,' was Simon's polite reply. 'You see, I have just completed a book on the subject myself.'

What, he was asked rather condescendingly, was the title of this book?

'Well, it is called the Simon Report,' answered the chairman of the commission appointed by Parliament.

Taken to extremes, the air of apparent detachment from affairs of state which is rather engaging in some politicians, totally silences others. The only recorded utterance in the Commons from Sir Isaac Newton during his spell as an MP was a request to have a window opened to let in a little fresh air.

Up in the Lords the Earl of Leicester rose to his feet in 1972 to tell his fellow-peers that he was about to break twenty-two years of silence in the chamber by taking part in a debate on pollution. He went on to explain that he had been following a tradition long observed in his family. His father had been a member of the House for twenty-three years and had never spoken in a debate; neither had his grandfather, who had sat in the Lords for thirty-two years; nor indeed had his great-grandfather whose term as one of their lordships had run an impressive sixty-seven years.

Setting a supreme example to high and low in the land comes the Royal Family, of course. Their attention to duty was admirably commended by Lord Derby, speaking at the inaugural dinner of the British Industries Fair many years ago, when he told his listeners, 'Hour after hour they go round and round showing an honesty of purpose I should like many of my horses to have.'

Slightly similar is Geoffrey Madden's definition of Peers to the Realm: 'A kind of eye-shade or smoked glass, to protect us from the full glare of Royalty.'

The Abdication may have rocked the nation but a rapid return to normal was marked on only the third day after George VI's accession when he announced that he intended keeping up the royal racing stables, which his elder brother had viewed with indifference.

Members of the Royal Family set standards to all their subjects in times of adversity too. Not long after the outbreak of the last war the *Daily Sketch* gave the gentle reproach, 'Lazy girls should be jogged by the mention that the Duchess of Kent is doing her own nails.'

And this selfless attitude to work rubs off on others as a member of the Royal Household once explained: 'Being an extra Lady-in-Waiting means that one doesn't have too many extra engagements to perform, which is just as well since I have this house in Chelsea, my father-in-law's house in Scotland, and a house in Mustique to keep running. I really wouldn't want another house, you know. I think there is such a thing as being overhoused.'

It may be because the Royal Family set such a praiseworthy example in their working lives that some of their most meticulous subjects feel they can point out minor flaws. 'There must have been a number of retired officers and other ranks who raised an eyebrow on seeing pictures of the Queen – in uniform – carrying Prince Andrew', wrote an old army man to the *Daily Mirror*. 'Even in plain clothes, before the war, it was not "done" for an officer to be seen carrying even the smallest parcel.'

Still, Her Majesty can doubtless be consoled by the thought that old soldiers of this mentality frequently fall into the category of the fellow-officer whose confidential report one year contained this comment on his approach to his work: 'Men will follow this officer – if only out of sheer curiosity.'

FAIR
PLAY

We British may not always have been the world's best in international sporting competitions, but there was a time when our approach to sport closely mirrored the tenor of national life. Even today it's still a revealing social barometer, although the idea that time spent on school playing fields sets us up for the greater game of life doesn't hold much water these days. That's unless you're heading for a career as a sporting superstar, but it's hardly the same thing as the civilizing training for life that playing games was once held to be.

Sir Fred Burrows, the last Governor of Bengal before Indian independence, was a graphic example of the changes that were coming about in British public life after the war, as the old order was broken up, leaving monoliths of the traditional establishment to drift about like icebergs, occasionally colliding with things until they melted away and disappeared. 'Unlike my predecessors,' he told an Indian audience in one of his speeches, 'I have devoted more of life to shunting and tooting than to hunting and shooting.'

What they made of it is anyone's guess, but Lord Curzon's response to a former President of the NUR running part of his domain makes amusing conjecture.

The importance of playing the game and the game you played used to be one of the most significant factors in distinguishing your rung on the social ladder. It had important spin-offs in the field of employment.

Admiral Sir Charles Carpentdale, an early Deputy

Director General of the BBC, made a point of asking each candidate for any of the more important posts in the Corporation the searching question, 'What games do you play?' Promising careers could be nipped in the bud by an inopportune answer.

Games have always been important in service life; so has hunting – even in the Royal Navy. The speaker at an annual Hunt Breakfast of the Britannia Beagles before the war told his audience, 'It would be an unhappy day for the future of the Senior Service if the beagles failed to function. Hunting teaches sound sporting qualities, and enables cadets to go forth into all parts of the world as ambassadors for their country.'

The thrill and schooling of the chase isn't neglected on active service either. It's said that the Duke of Wellington insisted on hunting regularly during his campaigns and when the 1st King's Dragoon Guards found themselves chasing terrorists in Palestine, they sought a little light relief by maintaining a pack of hounds, and hunting the local quarry, clad in pink coats and velvet caps under the Middle Eastern sun.

This approach to sport by the British gentleman had obviously beneficial influences to its supporters. Viewing the grave situation in Europe as fascism gained a tighter grip, one Colonel Lowther, a member of the Pytchley, suggested, 'I think that if we could get the dictators to come out with the Pytchley Hounds, their attitudes towards life might change considerably. They would get a better idea of the real meaning of friendship.' (Though not, one presumes, from the fox.)

Joining him in this sentiment was a Cambridgeshire MP, speaking at a bowls dinner in Cambridge, who suggested, 'If only Hitler and Mussolini could have a good game of bowls once a week in Geneva, I feel that

Europe would not be as troubled as it is.' Bowls, it must be remembered, were awfully handy when it came to seeing off the Spanish Armada.

Sport was also seen in the vanguard of civilization. 'Where else except in Kenya,' asked a correspondent to the *Hampshire Chronicle*, 'could an African whose grandparents were perhaps cannibals watch really good polo?'

It helped the defence of civilization. During a race meeting at Cheltenham the editor of the *Gloucestershire Echo* received a letter from an ardent race-goer in defence of racing, which contained the statement, 'You, sir, will entirely agree with me that rugby, Association football, boxing and racing are a buttress against Bolshevism and other prevailing evils of the day.'

One evening in the early 1950s prisoners in the open prison at Leyhill were treated to a talk given by the Duke of Beaufort on the duties of the Master of Horse and on Foxhunting, which they no doubt found most enlightening. How it helped their rehabilitation went unrecorded, but perhaps it was seen as setting them back on the right scent, so to speak.

In the wider world of politics the training and discipline that a gentleman acquired from his quest for sporting prowess was bound to stand him in good stead in the great game that followed. You didn't have to be British either to appreciate this.

When King George II of Greece was driven out of his country in 1923, only a year after his succession, one of the abiding memories that sustained him through the years of poverty and exile until his return in 1935 was being bowled first ball in a cricket match while he'd been at school in England. This, he used to tell his friends, helped him to treat his expulsion as a stepping stone to final triumph.

If sport could intrude into politics the reverse was also true, and not just in the case of the Olympics. Ian Fleming's explorer brother, Peter, was reckoned to be one of the finest shots of his day and his game-book records many memorable days out with his gun. One of these was 14 November 1947, when seven guns, including George VI, had bagged 549 pheasants. 'Splendid day,' wrote Peter Fleming in his remarks column, 'all wild birds and mostly very good. H.M. very accurate. Everyone in good form over Dalton's resignation.' (The Labour Chancellor of the Exchequer had only recently resigned after inadvertently leaking details of his Budget to a journalist.)

Indeed, in the higher circles of the British Establishment, the suggestion that you had no interest in sports, or worse still were deliberately unfit for them, could be damning. It's for that reason that poor Viscount Haldane, who as Secretary for War founded the Territorial, found himself walking to Brighton one night when by rights he should have been tucked up in bed.

He'd been enjoying a convivial meal with some of his peers when the conversation turned lightheartedly to his considerable girth. Haldane bridled at this, maintaining that just because he was generously upholstered it didn't necessarily follow that he was out of condition and to prove the point he volunteered to set off immediately to walk to Brighton, sixty miles away, dressed in his evening clothes. Furthermore, he told his dining companions that he wouldn't allow himself more than two minutes' rest in every hour and promised to send them a telegram as soon as he arrived. He then rose from the table and did precisely that.

In the eyes of the gentleman, playing the game for its own sake has always been of far greater importance than the mere lust for victory. Neville Lytton, who balanced his artistic temperament by excelling at tennis (both real and lawn), enjoyed telling of the occasion at Cannes when he was competing in a lawn tennis tournament and was told by the captain of the American Davis Cup team, 'I can't make it out; you always seem to have a smile on your face, and you seem equally pleased whether you win or lose.'

'Mr Hardy,' Lytton replied, 'those who have no ambitions have no disappointments.'

All the same he was honest enough to admit that he didn't always live up to this ideal and he thanked real tennis, the version that Henry VIII used to play so energetically in his youth, for reminding him of how he should approach the game. Neville Lytton was a good player, good enough to become amateur champion, and he recalled the early round of one championship when he won eighteen games in a row from an opponent. When he came off court, Covey, one of the best players of the game, blew him up 'like a pickpocket', to use Lytton's own inventive phrase. He went on to recall, 'He pointed out to me that if an opponent was not of my class I must handicap myself – knock off all difficult services, play only the openings, and somehow or other make the game have a semblance of genuine equality.'

In his view it was the strong traditions of chivalry inherent in real tennis that meant there was 'no finer training of manners in the world'.

As someone recalled a few Wimbledons ago, 'how

different that tournament would be today if Connors and McEnroe were Wykehamists'.

Admittedly Neville Lytton was describing an attitude of mind at the turn of this century and not the million-dollar business of the professional tennis circuit eighty years later, but it's still reassuring to find that elements of his world survive.

Once in a while there's a brief report of real tennis competition hidden in the sporting pages of the *Daily Telegraph* or *The Times*, and *Country Life* has been known to run a full page on the championships in some years. Set alongside its historic traditions and absurdly complex rules and scoring system, squash seems a very humble relation, but what entrepreneur is throwing up real tennis complexes today? Aye, there's the rub.

Winning with a good grace is also terribly important. Bowling underarm to win a vital match just isn't – even if you're Australian – well, cricket. Nor is going over the top when you clinch victory in any game. A letter printed in the *Telegraph* some time ago summed up this fundamental hallmark of good breeding:

When I watch modern soccer players, long-haired and emotional as a lot of hysterical women, kissing each other when they score a goal, it reminds me of an incident on the polo ground at Secunderabad in 1922. I was lucky enough to score the goal that won the cup and started waving my polo stick in the way that a Zulu used to wave his assegai during battle. The Second in Command of my Regiment quietly called me over as captain of the team and impressively said, 'You should remember there are losers.' A lesson I never forgot. When he died a

couple of years ago, I sent that incident to his vicar
in a Berkshire village as my tribute to a great English
sportsman. The vicar read it out at the service.

It's when people start to take the games too
seriously (some would go as far as saying when they
start to practise for them) that they lose their simple
appeal. In a line worthy of Oscar Wilde, Herbert
Spencer once remarked to a young man with whom he
was playing billiards, and who had just made a break of
one hundred, 'Young fellow, a certain ability at games
is a graceful thing, but skill such as yours is evidence of
a misspent youth.'

Money is often blamed for spoiling the sheer fun of
amateur games, but it can't be held to blame entirely.
During Fred Perry's heyday on the tennis court a
headline appeared with the delightfully ambivalent
news, 'Perry to remain an amateur if he can make
£20,000.'

For all his love of the amateur code Neville Lytton
was blind to reality. Even in his day top sportsmen
were making money from writing for the press. His
fellow tennis player, Eustace Miles, regularly wrote an
article entitled 'How I Won the Championship'
(sometimes changed to 'How I Lost the Championship').

The distinction between amateur and professional
was rather subtle when it came to winnings from lawn
tennis. According to Neville Lytton it was customary
to be awarded a voucher at a jeweller, on the
assumption that if you bought luxuries your amateur
status wasn't jeopardized. Buying life's necessities at
once ranked you as a professional.

Apparently some debate was caused among the

Lawn Tennis Association when Elizabeth Ryan, the American winner of nineteen titles at Wimbledon, saved up all her winnings and used these to buy a car. I suppose that was still considered to be a luxury, because the LTA allowed her to keep it and remain within the laws of the game. However, when Max Decugis, joint winner of the men's doubles at Wimbledon in 1911, used part of his prize to buy a sack of potatoes there was a storm of disapproval. It all seemed quite illogical.

Charles Burgess Fry was another amateur sportsman cast in the traditional mould. Many years after his sporting triumphs and well into his seventies, he confided to a friend that he was toying with the idea of opening racing stables and getting involved with the Turf. 'In what capacity, Charles,' asked his friend, 'trainer, jockey or horse?'

In 1927 the author of *Etiquette for Men* had a word or two for his readers on the correct approach to sports and games:

> The golden rule in sport of any kind is always to 'play the game'. If you remember this, you will have no difficulty in obeying the many little 'unwritten laws' of sport as readily as the established rules of the game.

If you don't happen to understand this principle, then the chances of breaking the 'unwritten laws' are as great as they were for a Middle-Eastern oil potentate who decided to exercise his sporting rights over his recently acquired country seat in England and set off to bag a few pheasants. Unfortunately no one had thought to mention that it was customary to use a twelve-bore rather than a machine-gun.

Fishing is another of the gentleman's traditional sports that has suffered from money, in the form of a steep rise in prices, not to mention a marked decline in fish. (Although game fishing is still the preserve of the well-to-do, fishing in general is of course the one field sport most infiltrated by the lower orders.)

Fishermen's tales abound, but those concerned with the affluent side of the sport have more than a ring of financial reality. There was the wealthy angler who took himself off to one of the best stretches of salmon river in Scotland, fished for a fortnight and landed one miserable four-pounder on his last day. As he looked at the pathetic fruit of his two weeks' endeavour he said to his ghillie, 'You know that fish has cost me two thousand pounds!'

'Ah, well. Be grateful you only caught the one,' came the reply.

The scarcity of fish, coupled with the outrageous prices demanded to catch them, can sometimes lead to anglers exaggerating the size of those they do hook; not the act of a gentleman, perhaps, but an indication of the pressure that money can bring to bear on the most peaceful of pastimes.

Another angler in Scotland was asked by the mother of a week-old baby if she could borrow his scales to weigh her wee one, now that he was home from hospital. She lived in a remote croft, far from her post-natal clinic and was keen to see how her baby was progressing. The fisherman was a little reluctant but, in the absence of any convincing reason for refusing her request, handed over his spring balance. The baby was placed in a towel which was hung from the balance and to the mother's astonishment the scale registered a weight of twenty-eight pounds.

'What an extremely well-nourished child,' observed the angler without a flicker of surprise as he hurriedly repacked his balance and set off in search of another spot to try his fly.

Cricket is probably the one game in which men of all classes have met, if not on equal terms, at least in a manner that has enabled everyone to enjoy the game. The old Gentleman and Players matches enshrined the distinction between the upper and lower orders and permitted this mixing to take place.

The division, so clear to an English mind, left foreign visitors baffled. An American taken by his English host to watch a game at Lords asked him to explain the meaning of 'Gentlemen vs Players' on the fixture list.

'Actually, it's our way of saying Amateurs vs Professionals,' replied the Englishmen.

As they were leaving, the American noticed the sign 'Gentlemen' at various places around the ground and asked his host this time, 'Tell me, what do the professionals do?'

It was another American who, after watching a few overs at The Oval, explained why cricket isn't a game likely to make great headway in his home country. 'Now I see what it is,' he said to the man who had brought him. 'Just a few friends and no flowers.'

Taking my younger son's American godfather, the splendid Roosevelt van Williams, to his first cricket match at Lord's, we arrived at a particularly tense moment of a test match between England and Australia. We sat together in the stand. The suspense was unbearable. After some fifteen minutes he whispered in my ear, 'Are you allowed to talk?'

Neville Cardus, for all his devotion to the game, admitted, 'There is one great similarity between cricket and music. There are slow movements in both.'

In spite of that, his namesake, Neville Lytton once again, embodied the noble spirit of the national game when he wrote:

> Village cricket is the thing. Here the squire, the butcher, the parson, the undertaker, the Socialist, the Tory all meet on a footing of delightful equality ... The varieties of form are neutralized by the vagaries of the pitch, and there is an atmosphere of guileless good fellowship that is typical of a great and lovable race.

He may not have approved of young men spending six days a week out of every summer playing cricket at a time when the country was girding itself for war, but he thoroughly supported this carefree blending of high and low which was to be so vital when it came to the sterner business of knocking the Hun for six.

These values were still evident at a time of even greater adversity, when the old country was really up against it and the tattered remnants of the British Expeditionary Force were clustering on the beaches of Dunkirk. A cricket Blue who recalled his experience of the evacuation said that one of the things that impressed him most was that it would have been possible to pick two first-class Gentlemen vs Players sides.

As you might expect, the view of cricket wasn't quite the same from the Players' side of the fence. During a match between Oxford University and Lancashire, an immaculately clad undergraduate was called to the wicket. Walking crisply from the pavilion, he politely acknowledged the two umpires, took his guard, surveyed the field appraisingly and settled down to receive the first ball. This removed his off stump with surgical precision and off he set again back to the pavilion, walking smartly and erect. 'That was a very fine ball,' he said to one of the outfielders as he passed.

'Aye, but it were wasted on thee,' was the reply.

Judging by some reports, village cricket hasn't necessarily been everything Neville Lytton might have wished. W.G. Grace took part one afternoon in a charitable match against a village club in his home county of Gloucestershire, and a large crowd gathered to watch the famous man at the wicket. The opposing wicketkeeper rather fancied himself, and set his heart on stumping the world's most celebrated player. The third ball of Grace's first over gave him his chance and, whipping off the doctor's bails, he cried 'Owzat!' in triumph.

Grace was preparing to return to the pavilion when the umpire answered coldly, 'Very smart! Very smart, indeed! But don't let me catch you doing it again. These people have come to see Dr Grace bat; not to see you keep wicket.'

National interest in the game may have declined along with the fortunes of English Test sides but there was a time, and not so long ago, when the BBC gave cricketing success precedence over industrial news. At Christmas 1954 the first item to be announced on one news broadcast was the English victory in the second Test at Sydney. After this sweetener came the report that the NUR had just decided to call a strike on the railways.

Then there was the parish priest, worried by the

drought that was threatening crops in his area, who told a colleague that he was going to offer up a prayer for rain at morning service the following Sunday, and wondered whether he might think of doing the same. The next day the second priest had a call asking him to hold back for a week. 'Not next Sunday,' his friend told him. 'Hold on until the Sunday after. I don't think we should do anything that might spoil the Test match.'

Rugby, with its division into Union and League, has never had the same power of national bonding as cricket. 'The behaviour of spectators at some Rugby matches has declined,' wrote a disillusioned enthusiast to the *Daily Sketch*, 'just as now a lot of the wrong people play. Rugby used to be played only at better class schools. To attempt to lump Rugby, the game and the spectators with the thousands of layabouts at the soccer grounds is quite useless, as it is to compare the amateur game with the professional, with its wages, absurd transfer fees and now, God help us, talks of strikes.'

The dividing lines can be sharply drawn even in Rugby Union. A Welsh team up to play against a leading London club found themselves one man short and were about to field only fourteen players when the London captain knocked politely at the door of their changing-rooms and said to his opposite number in the reassuring tones of a leading public school, 'I hear you're a man short, old chap. If you like, we'd be very happy to lend you one of our reserves.'

'Oh, no, there's no need,' replied the Welshman, beaming, 'we don't intend being one man down for too long.'

Once upon a time golf was the preserve of a

privileged elite, which fostered the remark in a Sunday newspaper, 'The inspiring fact that dominates golf is that it is a game for gentlemen and gentlewomen to play. The others who play it need not be considered.' Thank you very much!

Supporting this is the story of the highly respected barrister who had long cherished the hope of playing one of the most exclusive courses in the Home Counties.

He duly presented himself to the secretary one day, named his own well-respected club and asked if he might be allowed to play a round.

'Guest of a member?' asked the secretary.

'No, sir.'

'Then I'm afraid not.'

As the barrister was leaving the clubhouse he noticed the familiar figure of a High Court Judge reading his paper. Approaching him, the barrister asked deferentially whether he might be allowed to play the course as the judge's guest.

Putting down his paper, the judge eyed him closely and asked, 'Religion?'

'Church of England, sir.'

'Education?'

'Eton, sir. Then Oxford. Firsts in Mods and Greats. Winner of the Gaisford.'

'Games?'

'Rugby, sir, rackets, and rowed two in the winning Boat Race crew.'

'Army?'

'Grenadier Guards, sir, Major. MC and *Légion d'Honneur*.'

'Actions?'

'Dunkirk, Alamein, Normandy, sir.'

The judge nodded gravely, pondering his decision, and then nodded to the club secretary, saying, 'Nine holes.'

If you were searching for exclusive sporting bodies at the turn of the century, there can't have been many to match the Public Schools Alpine Sports Club, which by its name and nature excluded all but a well-heeled and leisured minority. Even so it happened one year that the cup awarded for skating was won by a lady who spoke with what the members took to be a Cockney accent. This episode caused a flurry of consternation and extraordinary meetings were called to ensure that nothing so frightful could ever happen again.

One field in which women were allowed to triumph was racing, again because its financial exclusivity guaranteed that only the right sort would emerge the winners. Not that these ladies actively participated in the race; they were the horses' owners. All the same, in the year when horses owned by women came in first and second in the Derby it was hailed by the *Daily Telegraph* as such 'a triumph for feminism as it has not won since the Cambridge examiners placed a woman above the Senior Wrangler'. Now, you can't say more than that.

The last word on the nation's attitude to sport ought to go to Lord Rosebery, who played a leading part in running and reforming the English Turf and who counted a number of famous horses in his stable. Speaking about the state of the nation itself on one occasion, he commented, 'I would point out one thing first, that the aim of everyone in this country is to breed the winner of the Derby.'

HOW GREEN IS MY VALET

'I WILL ONLY WORK FOR A GENTLEMAN,' DECLARED A living Jeeves. 'I don't have to interview my future employer to establish whether he is one or not. The moment I walk into his presence I can *feel* whether he is a gentleman.'

Confidence like this may be reassuring for true blues, but for anyone keen to cover the traces of their own ancestry, it's decidedly unsettling and demoralizing. As the ultimate social litmus test, however, experienced criticism of this sort is the last word and an unfavourable impression can be damning in a seasoned eye.

During one of his spells under an alias, T.E. Lawrence was assigned as a batman to an officer drawn from the category which in wartime had been cruelly classified as 'temporary gentlemen'. Like the butler above, Lawrence felt instinctively that while his superior may have been an officer he was certainly no gentleman, and he formed an instant and vitriolic loathing for the wretched man.

On their first evening together as Lawrence was unpacking the officer's kit he remarked, 'I beg your pardon, sir, but I can only find one of your razors.'

'I've only got one razor,' replied the other.

'Indeed, sir? I thought most gentlemen had a razor for every day of the week.'

The unpacking continued for a minute or two before Lawrence put his next question: 'Sir, I can't find your left-handed nail scissors.'

That effectively ended their brief relationship and Lawrence hastily transferred to duties more to his liking.

In circumstances where a gentleman's gentleman finds a master who does meet with his approval, the relationship established between them can be very touching. On the morning when the late Lord Tredegar was taken seriously ill his valet, Cronin, entered his master's bedroom as usual and was greeted with the words, 'Cronin, I think I'm dying,' in place of his customary nod of recognition. 'The habit of years could not be broken in me,' recalled Cronin, 'and I knew that Lord Tredegar in his more collected moments would not wish it to be.' So he simply answered, 'Very good, my lord,' which ensured that the customary silence between them at that hour was restored, to the comfort of both.

Fifty years ago the Duke of Marlborough reflected a similar dependence on his right-hand man. Staying with one of his daughters, and for once without his valet, he appeared at breakfast on his first morning complaining that his toothbrush wasn't frothing as it normally did and asking if someone could get him a replacement. It had to be pointed out to him tactfully that unless he used the tooth powder, normally applied every morning by his man, no toothbrush would froth to his satisfaction.

By the same token the civic authorities in Birmingham felt the need to advertise for a butler in order to relieve the Lord Mayor of the chore of pouring drinks himself whenever he offered his guests a glass of something.

Maintaining the dividing line between fond respect and too close an intimacy has always been a vital element in any successful relationship between the serving and served. When it breaks down, embarrassing complications can arise. An elderly spinster whose long-serving chauffeur had to be admitted to hospital for minor surgery went to visit him and was asked by the ward sister whether she was his wife. 'Certainly not,' answered the lady. 'I am his mistress.'

Nevertheless, correct form may still hold true even in the most intimate circumstances, as happened to the young daughter of one of our noble families when she took more than a shine to a dashing steward while sailing out to South Africa. Their passion reached its height at a fancy-dress ball held towards the end of the voyage in which they managed to spend most of the evening together without arousing suspicion, before they retired to the lady's cabin.

The steward had to be on duty at six to prepare for breakfast and it wasn't until later in the morning that he managed to catch up with his lady love whom he'd left sleeping peacefully. His ardour was soon cooled though as she greeted his affectionate 'Good morning,' with the remark, 'In the circles in which I move sleeping with a woman does not constitute an introduction.'

Misunderstanding and embarrassment can arise from other forms of mistaken identity. On one occasion the Earl of March lent a hand in running a conference which required him to meet a lorry carrying special equipment for it very early on the first morning. At six-fifteen he was standing on the pre-arranged spot to meet the driver and give directions. Right on time the lorry pulled up and his lordship hailed the driver cheerfully and asked him to drive through a couple of side-streets to the back of the conference building where he'd be waiting for him.

'Just a moment, governor,' answered the man. 'Who are you?'

'I am,' replied his lordship with some diffidence, 'the ... the Earl of March.'

'In that case I'm the Earl of April,' scoffed the driver.

From the days of hansom cabs comes the story of Lord Rothschild hiring a cab to take him home one evening. Alighting at his door he paid the cabby and presented him with what he thought was a perfectly reasonable tip. The cabby thought otherwise, and after pocketing the coin rather disdainfully informed his fare, 'I've often driven your lordship's son home and he always gives me a good deal more than you've done.'

'I daresay he does,' answered Lord Rothschild. 'But then, you see, he has got a rich father: I haven't!'

At the time when many domestic staff were dressed in clothes not dissimilar to those of the diners whom they served, there were frequent complaints from the less initiated about the risk of mistaking a guest for a servant and vice versa. The author of a book of etiquette at the end of the last century offered a ready solution which put paid to this anxiety:

It is not necessary to have a distinguishing dress for a waiter. If a gentleman is a gentleman, no one is likely to mistake him for a waiter, and if he is not a gentleman, what does it matter if the mistake is made?

Unfortunately the pious theory was less straightforward in practice, as was demonstrated in an awkward incident involving a member of Curzon's staff at the

Lausanne Conference in 1922. The man had recently been recruited as his lordship's valet and only after they had arrived in Switzerland did it become apparent that he drank – heavily.

One night he appropriated some of his master's evening clothes and took to the floor in the ballroom of the Beau Rivage Hotel, as high as a kite and having a rare old time with the delegates' wives.

Curzon ordered him home on the first train, which he duly caught – though not before exacting his revenge.

The following morning Curzon found that his erstwhile valet had removed every pair of his trousers, leaving him with only the evening trousers he'd worn the night before. There was just an hour before the conference was to be convened and Curzon's staff made desperate calls to try and apprehend the fugitive at the frontier. In the meantime the valet's room was turned inside out but revealed nothing but the empty bottles he'd drained before quitting.

In blank despair, Harold Nicolson, who was with Curzon at the time, sat down heavily on the bed and discovered the valet's cache. Under the counterpane lay all of the missing trousers, carefully sandwiched into a trouser press!

On occasions it was sometimes necessary for considerate employers to advance their servants clothes, which it was generally accepted they would inherit when their masters had finished with them. Lieutenant-Colonel Jacques Balsan, who married Consuelo Vanderbilt after her divorce from the ninth Duke of Marlborough, had to help his valet out of a tight spot while they were visiting Blenheim on one occasion. His man complained that the other valets staying there were scornful of his blue serge suit, so to help him to keep up appearances in the servants' quarters, Balsan lent him a dinner jacket.

A curious paradox over clothing arose in a particularly exclusive nudist club where it was decided that in spite of the natural state enjoyed by the members, all the club's servants should remain fully clothed. Members who obviously raised no objection to seeing fellow-members in the altogether, said they took a very dim view of being waited on by staff similarly disrobed!

The attitude taken by employers to their own staff reveals a great deal about their 'nobility' in its broadest sense. The Marchioness of Londonderry, one of the most intimidating society ladies of her day, found a very junior parlour maid trying each of the chairs in her drawing-room in turn when she re-entered having said goodbye to afternoon tea guests. The look of horror on the poor girl's face showed that she was expecting a sound ticking off at the discovery, but her mistress summed up the situation in a flash. Edward VII had been among the company that had just departed. 'That was the chair the King sat on,' she told the maid with uncharacteristic gentleness. 'Sit down on it.'

Employers recently elevated to this station can't be counted on to display the same sensitivity; nor can those who dish out advice to them. The author of *Planning Your Home for Tomorrow* came up with the suggestion, 'There is no reason why the laundry should not also contain the servants' bath. A servants' bath will be used only occasionally.'

There was the employer who admitted to living 'very quietly, with a staff of seven domestics' who saw

SYMPATHETIC

Young wife (rather nervously)   *Oh, cook, I must
really speak to you. Your master is always complaining.
One day it is the soup, the second day it is the fish, the
third day it is the joint — in fact, it is always something or
other.*
Cook (with feeling)   *Well, mum, I'm truly sorry for
you. It must be quite* **hawful** *to live with a gentleman of
that sort.*

the extension of domestic service as a practical solution
to the unemployment of the 1930s. Yet as he, or she,
pointed out, in spite of the many thousands of girls and
women looking for work, there didn't seem to be any
household servants available; finding a kitchenmaid, in
particular, seemed to be quite impossible.

Another, writing to the *Herts and Essex Observer*,
complained,

> For years now in England servants have been
> growing scarcer. Should war break out the flight to
> the factories would make us almost destitute of
> domestic help of any kind. And, yet, nothing is done
> about it – except the grumbling.

On a sizeable country estate less than fifty years ago
the occupants of a number of tied cottages took their
drinking water from a ditch, while their landlord's
pheasants had thoughtfully been supplied with piped
water.

In much the same way, when the marvels of modern
technology presented the people of Saxby-All-Saints
on Humberside with the possibility of an electricity
supply, the local squire and owner of the three-
thousand-acre estate vetoed the idea. Many of the
villagers too claimed that they preferred to remain
lightening their darkness with the friendly glow of oil
lamps that had served the village for generations. To
any voices raised in surprise at this decision, the clerk
to the council had a ready answer: 'The question of
electricity in our homes is not the parish council's
affair. We must accept the squire's decision.'

At this period, the last excesses of Victorian bigotry
were also being worked out at another large country

WHAT WILL BECOME OF THE SERVANT-GALS?

Charming lady (showing her house to benevolent old gentleman) *That's where the housemaid sleeps.*
Benevolent old gentleman *Dear me, you don't say so! Isn't it very damp? I see the water glistening on the walls.*
Charming lady *Oh, it's not too damp for a servant.*

seat where the head gardener was required to wear a tie throughout the year, no matter how hot it was. He was also banned from smoking, as were the under-gardeners. In fact anyone caught enjoying a quick puff was given his cards on the spot. It was also forbidden for any gardener to be seen in the house, and the very junior garden staff who helped with the flower decorations inside the principal rooms had to creep about shortly after dawn without making a sound. As a final indignity it was ruled that none of the garden staff were allowed to look at the lady of the house as she drove about the grounds in her motorized chair!

Set against absurd cases like this are those incidents of genuine, if grudging, respect, which stem from a mutual regard established between man and master. A striking example of this occurred on a bitterly cold afternoon in Norfolk, when a peppery old landowner out shooting shortly before the Great War hit a pheasant which dropped into a frozen pond. The spaniel beside him sniffed the icy fringe and ventured no further, preferring the heat of its master's rage to the numbing chill of the water. So he bellowed at his gamekeeper to plunge in and fetch the bird.

'Shan't,' retorted the man indignantly.

'Quite right,' replied his master, collecting himself after the momentary outburst. 'I'd have thought you a fool if you had.'

True countrymen have a healthy respect for the right sort of casual labour as well. 'If I ever wanted rough work done quickly and cheaply', advised an old hand in *Countryman*, 'give me the tramp navvy. Sub him every night, pay him a penny or two over the local rate, put a ganger over him, and you can work him sixteen hours a day.'

But these are cases drawn from the closing years of a bygone age. Today the approach to service is markedly different. Minds broaden for one thing.

Thirty years ago when the young Viscount Throwley was sailing round the world on a 200-ton schooner he was able to report, 'We have two cockney crew members who are most amusing. They call me "Lordy". One wouldn't expect that from servants at home, of course, but abroad I don't mind.'

In the same vein was the rather more disgruntled

comment by a passenger lunching in a British Rail restaurant car, who was assailed by a waiter asking cheerfully, 'Do you gents want something to drink?' In the passenger's view this was not 'the right way for a wine waiter to address First Class passengers'.

And what about VIP passengers addressing rail staff? Once again the Royal Family have the right answer, as a steward on the royal train confided: 'When Prince Andrew comes aboard he always comes to the galley and waves at us and shouts, "Hallo slaves" – only as a joke of course. The Royal Family treat you like a person.'

DREAMS
OF
EMPIRE

WHEN CHARLES DICKENS WAS CONTEMPLATING A VISIT to America in 1845, Lady Holland did her best to put him off the idea and suggested as an alternative, 'Go down to Bristol and see some of the third or fourth class people, they'll do just as well.'

For those who did venture overseas the 1902 edition of *Etiquette for Women* had this suggestion:

> That English people are absurdly conventional there is no denying; but when travelling it is their duty to lay aside some of their conventionality, and their reserve, and their air of superiority. Convinced of that superiority they can afford to be gracious.

It's taken two world wars, the loss of an empire and serious commercial competition to dent this self-confidence, and yet vestiges still linger on. If the British upper classes saw it as their duty to set an example to their lower orders, they felt an even greater responsibility to show foreigners the right way of going about things – an example that hasn't always been appreciated.

When Voltaire visited England he made a point of introducing himself to Congreve, but to the Frenchman's annoyance he found him far more concerned with being considered a gentleman than a playwright. This was quite incomprehensible to Voltaire who commented, 'If he hadn't written the plays, I should not have wished to make his acquaintance.'

The methods used to assert this superiority were more or less the same abroad as those maintained at home. Correct appearance was first and foremost. 'Having sailed extensively in European waters and visited most European ports, I can assure all British yachtsmen of the respect in which they are held everywhere', advised an unofficial ambassador. 'Those who go ashore to dine in ornately coloured shirts, shorts and plastic sandals, are not so much letting the side down as disappointing the local people by destroying their much-treasured image of the British yachtsman.'

The British winter sports enthusiast had other concerns awoken by notes of caution like this: 'The air of St Moritz is conducive to gaiety: the slightest amount of alcoholic refreshment when taken at a height of 5,000 feet is apt to cause lightheadedness, but luckily the control of one's behaviour is a prerogative of the Britisher.'

By following similar traditional pastimes of the well-to-do, the British abroad sought to maintain their unruffled appearance of complete confidence and calm continuity.

With something of an understatement, one of the contributors to *Rider* wrote in 1932:

At the moment the future of Shanghai does not look particularly bright, and whatever the outcome of the Sino-Japanese struggle it must be a long time before the social, to say nothing of the commercial, life of the port can recover. But if peace ever comes again it is sure that the Hunt will be one of the first activities of the European community to be put on its feet again.'

The same thought evidently occurred to General
Franco during the Spanish Civil War when he lifted a
temporary ban on hunting on Spanish territory and
allowed the garrison in Gibraltar to resume their sport
over land now controlled by him. In broadcasting this
news to the local populace the daily newspaper in
Seville told its readers that sport, especially hunting,
was a necessity to the British. It went on to mention
that the King was patron of the hunt and expressed the
hope that in future the British would look more
favourably on the Nationalist cause and, in view of
General Franco's generous concession, would cease
referring to him and his forces as 'insurgents'.

Whatever the merits, or otherwise, of spreading this
image abroad, it was unquestionably successful in
achieving its end. The English 'milord' became a
familiar and respected figure on the continent, and
avowed Anglophiles like the French art connoisseur
and diarist, Réné Gimpel, could define an English
gentleman in a couple of lines: 'A man with a passion
for horses, playing with a ball, probably one broken
bone in his body and in his pocket a letter to *The
Times*.'

The best of the landed classes were also recognized
for a quality that would have made them even prouder:
as valued and respected leaders.

A Russian lady who had suffered terribly during the
Bolshevik Revolution before making her escape, was
the guest at the Christmas revelries in a country house
owned by relatives of the English friends who had
offered her shelter. On her way to bed after the party
at which all the estate's retainers had been entertained
by the lord of the manor, she confided to her friends:
'When, and if ever, a revolution happens in England,

14 FEBRUARY

Mistress   *So you want me to read this love letter to you?*
Maid   *If you plaze, mam. And I've brought ye some*
cotton wool ye can stuff in yer ears while ye rade it!

and the people rise against their rulers, the farmers and
peasants of this estate will defend their landlord to the
last drop of their blood.'

Others might not have shown the same trust. When
Upstairs, Downstairs was first shown on American
television it was introduced by Alistair Cooke. He had
the difficult task of explaining to a disbelieving
American audience why English servants had not
murdered their masters long before the latter were
killed in the 1914–18 War.

It was hospitality which turned the tables, if only in
a small way, in the propaganda war waged between the

British and Germans in neutral Spain during the last war. At one stage, when the situation looked pretty bleak for Britannia, a member of the diplomatic staff threw a superlative cocktail party. Afterwards several influential and eminent Spaniards took him aside and said privately, 'Now we really know you are going to win the war.' For the rest of the hostilities the *entente* was very *cordiale*, in those quarters at least.

Stories told of German agents trying to pass themselves off as native-born Englishmen invariably concentrate on the minor solecisms they committed which gave them away. These range from the otherwise passable clone of a country gentlemen clad in Harris Tweed and cavalry twills, who blew his cover on only his first day by tucking into a picnic of Hunnish Wurst which he had shoved into his pocket before making his parachute jump, to those who'd managed to infiltrate more successfully before giving themselves away.

Among the most devious was the fellow who'd taken to smoking a pipe and playing golf at a respectable suburban golf club. However, he roused suspicions by betraying un-British behaviour when it was noticed that he ticked off his wife very harshly if she made a slip at bridge.

Dean Inge spoke for the majority of his countrymen when he reflected on national adversity: 'Never, even when the stormclouds appear blackest, have I been tempted to wish that I was other than an Englishman.'

There were those who preferred to express more formal thanks as in the case of the man whose will included the passage:

I desire to express my gratitude to Almighty God

for His many mercies, especially in sparing my life in
the railway catastrophe at Petit in Algeria, and for
the many privileges I have been allowed to enjoy,
including the prolongation of mind and body well
beyond the limit of threescore and ten, and of
having been born an Englishman in the reign of the
best of English sovereigns in the most interesting
and progressive of all periods of the world's history
under the most nearly perfect constitution and the
most beneficent and highly favoured Empire the
world has ever seen.

It was little wonder that the highest compliment
that could be paid a foreigner was to say that he was as
good as being English. Inevitably it was foreign royalty
who were singled out for this special honour. Writing
in his reminiscences, which carried the title *Old
Diplomacy*, Lord Hardinge of Penshurst paid a compliment to the last Czar of Russia, Nicholas II:

Much has been said about and written of the late
years of the unfortunate Emperor and Empress, but
I will say no more here than that the Emperor, had
he been an Englishman, would have been the most
perfect type of English gentleman.

While more recently King Leopold of the Belgians
was praised in a letter in the *Evening Standard* for being
'indistinguishable from an Englishman of the finest
type, so it comes as a surprise when he breaks into
fluent French'.

Mind you, not many Englishmen would have been
pleased if the same compliment had been paid to them
in reverse by the man in a foreign street. Understand-

ing a foreign language was one thing; speaking it like a native was never a trap that a self-respecting English gentleman would allow himself to fall into. The BBC was taken to task over this by a correspondent who firmly believed that foreign pronunciation of foreign names was merely an affectation. 'At home, if I talk French,' he continued, 'it is the French of Stratford-atte-Bowe, like Chaucer's Wife of Bath, and I wish the announcers would follow her example.' (If they had, there might have been more surprises: it was Chaucer's Prioress to whom the 'Frensh of Paris' was unknown – the Wife of Bath's claim to fame was her five husbands! But we can still sympathise with the complaint.)

The insidious usurping of English menus by the vocabulary of French cuisine was another cause of resentment to Englishmen deeply attached to the roast beef of old England. Among the objectionable foreign imports singled out by supporters of English cooking were: a saddle of Dorset lamb, which appeared on one menu as *La Selle d'Agneau de Dorset*; and the otherwise unassuming hashed mutton, which was dressed up in its French guise as *Agneau Hashish Parmentière*.

English menus aren't above adding a little colour to their simple homely fare, but there's frequently a dash of humour thrown in. I like the chalked blackboard in a pub that announced 'Chicken Surprise' among its list of goodies. Asked by a hungry customer what this delicacy was, the landlord answered without a flicker of expression, 'Lamb chop.' I don't suppose the Trades Description Act allows these little pleasantries nowadays.

Supreme among British statesmen with a cavalier approach to foreign tongues (which in reality didn't stray much further than French) stands Winston

Churchill. His command of that language was truly Anglo-Saxon, as was made evident during a visit to Clemenceau at Versailles. For reasons best known to himself Churchill turned up wearing the cap and jacket of an Elder Brother of Trinity House. Clemenceau made admiring comments about these and asked what uniform Churchill was wearing.

'Je suis un frère aîné de la Trinité,' he replied. To which Clemenceau is said to have responded, 'Mon Dieu! Quelle influence!'

Versailles was the setting for another sartorial exchange between Clemenceau and a British politician – this time A.J. Balfour. The two men arrived together for a garden party, Clemenceau wearing a bowler hat, Balfour a topper.

'They told me top hats would be worn,' remarked Balfour.

'They told me also,' said Clemenceau.

With behaviour like that coming from one of their national leaders it's hardly surprising that Englishmen harboured a deep suspicion, bordering on disdain at times, for the French and their institutions.

'What can you do,' asked an exasperated traveller, recently back from a holiday on the Riviera, 'with a nation who arrange all their plumbing so that hot water runs out of the tap marked "C"? I found this to be the case wherever I tried to wash my hands and in spite of numerous complaints no action was ever taken.'

Not many years ago a coroner who had cause to refer to the fact that the French drive on the opposite side of the road to the English, added, 'It seems to me a shame that they cannot make regulations on the Continent identical with those in this country.'

With attitudes as firmly entrenched as these the metric system was a non-starter and was dismissed by one sporting journalist because it meant nothing to most Englishmen, ruined their interest in races and worse still could 'never be accurate'.

And when it came to more intimate matters Field Marshal Montgomery voiced a common suspicion held by men of his generation during the passage of the Homosexuality Bill in 1965: 'This sort of thing may be tolerated by the French, but we are British — thank God.'

The *Sunday Pictorial* was delighted by an example of the 'British spirit at its best' during one of the periods of international tension that presaged the outbreak of the Second World War. This was given in the unlikely setting of the concert hall when James Whitehead, the cellist in the Philharmonic Trio, 'faced with one of those impossible modern foreign compositions which delight highbrows, said, "Oh, I can't play this thing," and walked off the platform.'

Sir Malcolm Sargent wasn't on much firmer ground with a member of Scandinavian royalty who attended one of his London concerts. The great conductor had a special fondness for rather grand patrons, and in the interval he hurried round to the Royal Box to present himself and his leading soloist. 'Your Majesty,' he announced, 'may I introduce Sergio Poliakoff? Sergio — the King of Norway.' The distinguished figure in the box shifted uncomfortably and murmured, 'Sweden.'

This unfamiliarity with foreign nobility is a revealing trait among the British Establishment who mix with them. Take the case of the society hostess who wanted to invite the Aga Khan to a glittering dinner she was planning, but had no idea where protocol demanded that he should sit. She turned to Debrett, who answered, 'The Aga Khan is considered by millions of his followers throughout the world to be directly descended from God. An English duke takes precedence.'

Abroad the British facility for remaining aloof and detached from the natives has had some unexpected spin-offs. It led one late Victorian guidebook to offer the comforting advice: 'It is a bad habit to run in a revolution – somebody might think you are "the other side" and shoot at you – but if you go calmly and look English there is no particular danger.'

It evidently persuaded an English tourist at Elsinore to place little faith in Danish weather forecasting. For during a tour of Hamlet's home which was sweltering in a temperature not far off ninety, this chap collapsed with heat-stroke and was taken to hospital. On admission, he was found to be wearing a winter overcoat, a tweed suit, two waistcoats, a full set of woollen underwear and a pair of mittens. He'd evidently put more trust in Shakespeare's references to the 'nipping and eager air' so favoured by the ghost of Hamlet's father as he haunted the nightwatch than in the thermometer. Though there's every likelihood that the deep-seated British suspicion and misunderstanding of Centigrade led him to believe that with a reading of thirty-two degrees, Elsinore in mid-July was literally freezing.

There's a rather charming naivety in this totally blinkered attitude which can extend even to public figures of a generally more enlightened disposition. Lady Astor peered into her crystal ball in search of a new world order and came up with the remarkable scenario, 'I would like China and Russia to be in the

framework of a new society formed by America and
the British Commonwealth, but they would have to
get into the British way of thinking.'

When America pipped us at the post by reaching
the moon ahead of the field one reader of the *Financial
Times* was still able to report optimistically, 'Britain
may not have been first on the moon, but at least we
lead the world in sewage treatment.'

His bright confidence was echoed by a member of
the British Winter Olympics team at Saporo in
February 1972 who remarked, 'We may not be the
greatest at winning Winter Olympics but at least we
can carry our bloody flag properly.'

On the subject of showing the flag, an old India
hand who offered hints to new arrivals in the
sub-continent quite cheerfully noted, 'Natives of India
think along different grooves of thought from ours. It
does not follow that we are always right. It is true,
however, that we are nearly always far more practical;
hence the need for us in the country.' After which he
gave five pages of lists of things to take with you
including half a dozen hats, one or more pairs of
knickerbockers, a complete set of cutlery for six and
three steel trunks of different sizes – practical advice
for one of the most challenging climates in the world!

I was told that the railway station in Kuala Lumpur
was completed to designs sent out by the British
Colonial Office. There the climate is equally challenging. The roof of the station was constructed to
withstand the weight of three feet of snow.

Yet it was this unflappable self-confidence, frequently pursued in the teeth of common sense, that
built the Empire.

Fifty years ago it was still possible for a missionary

to return from one of the wilder regions of His Majesty's domains, where native taste still clung enthusiastically to cannibalism, and report that although he hadn't yet succeeded in persuading the people to renounce the pleasures of this particular flesh, he had got as far as teaching them to use a knife and fork.

In Africa there was a District Commissioner who had the brainwave of leaving a glass eye in one of his villages to keep watch on the inhabitants. When they discovered that covering it blinded the eye to their transgressions the DC supplemented it with a pair of false teeth which carried the dire warning that they'd bite anyone who got within striking distance.

Old school ties were never far from view and the value of the gentleman's traditional grounding was clearly spelt out when Sir Peter Ramsbottom was appointed Governor of Bermuda. This posting so delighted one of his schoolfellows that he sent his congratulations to the island's people in having 'such an able and fair-minded administrator'. The chap knew what he was talking about too – he'd been Sir Peter's fag at Eton.

A bedrock of good taste has helped many British diplomats win respect abroad. The British Consul General in Warsaw at the outbreak of the Second World War was a fine example. Even among Poles he was regarded as an authority on their culture, from its literature to its cuisine. Among his many accomplishments he was greatly admired for the rare skill of distinguishing each of the country's 280 different kinds of vodka.

When things did turn sour and the harsh reality of war destroyed many dreams of empire, the truth was bitter indeed. With the invading Japanese Army sweeping down through the Malay peninsula, an English rubber planter who'd spent most of his life in the country, was seen smashing up his home before joining the retreat. He concentrated on his valuables, among them a lovingly decorated manuscript of Kipling's 'If'. This he destroyed with a hammer, poignantly reciting the verses with each blow.

My host at a recent dinner up-country from Johor Bahru would perhaps have appreciated the old planter's feelings. He would certainly have read Kipling. My invitation read, 'Black tie', which was somewhat surprising in a country with a constant temperature of some eighty-two to eighty-four degrees. I crossed the causeway from Singapore on a particularly sweltering night and after a long drive arrived at the planter's house. Inside the air-conditioning was turned to freezing and to my amazement I saw ahead of me in the drawing-room a blazing log fire. I huddled round it for warmth.

'Got to keep up the standards, old boy. Got to keep up the standards,' said the old planter, handing me a pink gin.

Kipling's message wasn't wasted. When the suggestion was made that German intelligence might be hoodwinked by broadcasting false forecasts about the weather at home, the worry was raised by a 'Lover of Truth' that this might be construed as lowering British standards to those of the enemy – a worthy case of being lied about, but not dealing in lies.

In the Gulf recently an old Arab friend told me that during the war they had been similarly plagued with German propaganda broadcasts. The area at the time was known as the Trucial States and was terribly pro-British. The wise old sheikh of Dubai, Sheikh

Rashid, was approached for his opinion as to whether the people should listen to the propaganda broadcasts. 'Of course,' said Sheikh Rashid. 'If the English hadn't wanted us to listen to the broadcasts, they wouldn't have invented wireless sets.'

As David Lloyd George once commented, 'The British Empire must behave like a gentleman.'

HIGH JINKS AND CURIOUS QUIRKS

GIVEN THAT A CONSIDERABLE AMOUNT OF INBREEDING must have taken place down the centuries in order to distill the blood blue into its present rich consistency, it's hardly surprising that a few eccentricities have developed among those in whose veins it flows. The upper classes have frequently earned a reputation for slightly curious behaviour, whether in boyish pranks or downright nonconformity.

The first category is most obviously represented by the riotous escapades of the young and prosperous while they are supposedly completing their studies. Originally this would have taken place at a university, but today embryo estate agents and the sons of wealthy landowners attending agricultural colleges are ranged alongside the ranks of the varsity undergraduates.

Location is immaterial; West End restaurants, the Badminton Horse Trials, the British Museum, or anywhere else you care to mention, may provide a suitable setting. What counts is spontaneity and style, leading to lots of jolly good fun, for the most part fairly innocent, and ideally at someone else's expense.

A typical example comes from the days when sanitation in our older universities still necessitated chamber pots. Living in a first-floor room overlooking a busy street was the high-spirited son of an earl. Beneath him resided an aged don, who had lived in the same set of rooms for half a century, apparently unconcerned by the hustle and bustle from the pavement outside his barred window.

One morning the young undergraduate was at a loss for something amusing to occupy him until his first glass of hock and seltzer at noon. It was a warm day, his window was open and the sound of the street outside drifted up through the casement, giving him an idea.

Tying a long piece of string to his pot, he lowered this out of his window until it was level with that of his elderly neighbour on the floor below. After a few outward jerks the pot started knocking against the old boy's window and a moment later the undergraduate was rewarded by seeing this open and an elderly arm reaching out to grab hold of the offending article. Once the handle was firmly in the old fellow's grasp, the undergraduate let go the string and watched for events to take their course.

He saw the elderly arm try to pull the pot through the bars into the room. Finding it too wide, it was tried vertically, but it still wouldn't pass through. Further attempts at various angles confirmed there was no chance of retrieving the chamber pot. This left two options. Either the pot was dropped and allowed to smash to pieces in the middle of a busy street, or else the old fellow had to hold on to it until help arrived. He chose to hang on.

Passers-by who couldn't help noticing the frail arm stretching out to them and gripping a huge receptacle had their consciences pricked and dropped in generous amounts of loose change as they walked by. Their bounty increased, and so did the weight of the pot, making it ever more difficult to hold and correspondingly less appropriate to be dropped.

The thanks with which the elderly fellow greeted the young man who lived above when he came to his aid quite eclipsed in his mind the origin of his unfortunate dilemma.

Carrying the torch for this worthy tradition comes Horace de Vere Cole, brother-in-law of Neville Chamberlain and acknowledged in his time as the king of practical jokers, who pursued his antics beyond his days at Cambridge and never really grew out of them.

His most celebrated pranks, the visit of the Sultan of Zanzibar to Cambridge (de Vere Cole himself hiding his undergraduate mien under an elaborate disguise) and the even more famous inspection of HMS *Dreadnought* by a group of Abyssinian dignitaries (this time represented by a group which included Virginia Stephen (later Woolf), with Cole as the man from the Foreign Office) both required a degree of pre-planning. Where his genius shone was in seizing the opportunity of the moment and extracting from it all the carefree fun at his disposal.

It was Horace de Vere Cole who first ran down a London street with a cow's udder protruding from his flies. It was he, too, who was credited with the surveyor spoof in which two passers-by were stopped by a man with a clip-board and asked to help by holding tight the end of a piece of string. One man was stopped round one side of a street corner, the second round the other side. Once each was in position, holding his end with strict instructions not to let it slacken, de Vere Cole disappeared with his clip-board and left them to it.

As a tall man with a commanding presence he found it easy to give instructions to others. Walking through London one morning he came across a gang of workmen equipped with tools and apparently awaiting the arrival of their foreman. With nothing much to do that day, Cole took charge and ordered the men to follow him. His little party made its way to Piccadilly, where Cole stopped them and began issuing instructions for marking out a large square in the road and a fair portion of the pavement. With these roped off, the men set to and began digging while Cole barked orders and kept them hard at it. He didn't neglect the policemen on point duty and under his stern tongue they were soon helping the congested traffic and thronging pedestrians to negotiate the road works.

At the end of the working day Cole checked that warning lamps had been set round what was now an impressive hole in one of London's busiest thoroughfares and then dismissed his men, telling them there was no need to return the following morning because another gang would be finishing off the job.

That was unquestionably true. The colossal hole continued to disrupt traffic well into the afternoon of the next day until the police began to wonder why no one was working on it. In fact it took a further twenty-four hours before the work was rectified and Piccadilly returned to normal, by which time the episode had probably completely slipped from Horace's mind.

Even his honeymoon didn't go unscathed. He took his bride to Venice, whose citizens he astonished on the morning of April Fool's Day by presenting them with little piles of horse manure dotted all round St Mark's Square. Undetected, he'd brought it by boat from a stable across the lagoon the night before. But the silent arriival and departure by water of so many horses kept Venetians guessing long into that spring day.

Following in Cole's footsteps come others of an

inventive disposition, among them the ill-fortuned
man with the surname Pierce Bottom. This had been a
source of inevitable ribaldry at school and university,
leading him to seek some form of redress from the
world at large. The scheme he hit on was to throw a
large dinner party for everyone else like him with a
'bottom' in their name. Thus Bottoms, Bottomleys,
Greenbottoms, Higginbottoms, Sidebottoms and Win-
terbottoms all over London were soon receiving

'Do you mind if we join in? — the food's terrible.'

elegantly printed invitations to a formal dinner at a
large West End Hotel. There they gathered in the
basement to be served rump steak. Their host failed to
turn up however, and his guests were even less amused
when each found he had to settle his own bill.

This propensity for practical jokes wasn't restricted
to overgrown Hooray Henrys. Leading members of the

British Establishment weren't above a little innocent fun now and again. The architect Sir Edwin Lutyens was one who relished childish practical jokes. Staying with the Sitwells once at Renishaw, he pulled a few strands of horsehair from a broken settee, folded them in a scrap of paper on which he had scribbled a few words and slipped the small package unnoticed into a desk drawer. This was discovered many years later by Osbert Sitwell, who read the note: 'A lock of hair from Marie Antoinette's hair, cut from her head ten minutes after execution.'

Refined, artistic temperaments like this are not infrequently tinged with a degree of harmless eccentricity which also helps to set apart those of a higher station. Such a man was John Christie, the founder of the Glyndebourne Festival Opera. Sixteen years as a master at Eton had left him with a passion for milk puddings (he'd been known to wolf down half a dozen helpings of tapioca at a sitting) and a love of English literature. This he used to share with the troops in the trenches of the Great War, reading extracts from such enduring favourites as Spenser's *Faerie Queene* and holding a question period at the end of each session.

Christie had an impish sense of fun which impelled him to write letters to *The Times* inspired by objects that attracted his curiosity. One was a kipper he'd just consumed for breakfast, which prompted the enquiry whether or not kippers were 'for want of a better term . . . left-handed', based on Christie's careful observation that some kippers had backbones on one side of their body, others backbones on the other side.

His sense of dress was unconventional too. In spite of owning 132 pairs of socks and 110 shirts at one time, he frequently teamed the white tie of his evening dress with a pair of well-worn tennis shoes. He also developed a great enthusiasm for lederhosen, and visitors to Glyndebourne in the summer of 1933, when this sartorial phase reached its peak, were expected to appear similarly attired.

John Christie was at ease in any society. Sitting next to the Queen at dinner once he removed his glass eye and polished it assiduously in his handkerchief for a minute or two before popping it back in and asking Her Majesty, 'In straight, Ma'am?' On the other hand he made it a habit always to travel third class whenever he took a train journey.

His attitude to music was less unconventional and his devotion to the works of Mozart was evident from

'I feel such a fool standing on Victoria Station in the middle of the afternoon.'

the Glyndebourne repertoire. Contemporary operas, though occasionally performed, were greeted with some reluctance – and not by Christie alone. Patrons wandering through the gardens during an interval in Hans Werner Henze's *Elegy For Young Lovers* came across Christie, an old man by this time, looking out across the fields. 'Do you see those cows off in the distance?' Christie asked. 'Well, when we do Mozart, they are always right here.'

Gerald Hugh Tywhitt-Wilson, fourteenth Baron Berners, shared Christie's love of music and his curious sense of fun. His family home at Faringdon, in what is today part of Oxfordshire, welcomed distinguished guests from many branches of the artistic world, though those who didn't know their host might have been perturbed by the signs around the estate which read, 'Dogs will be shot: cats will be whipped', or by the 140-foot-high tower that Lord Berners had had built on a nearby hill in 1935. That carried the warning: 'Members of the public committing suicide from this tower do so at their own risk.'

When last I visited Faringdon House there were doves encircling the portico – all dyed in wonderfully aesthetic pale greens, blues and pinks.

Among the guests was the ballet dancer Sir Robert Helpmann, who'd been asked to tea by Berners and was shown into the drawing-room to find Berners already enjoying the company of another guest – a horse. This he calmly fed scones while offering tea with sugar and/or cream to Helpmann. No reference was made to the horse's presence and only after its master had said that enough scones had been eaten was it led out of the room via the french windows. Much later in the conversation Helpmann raised the subject of their erstwhile companion.

'I'm very nervous,' his host explained. 'When people see the horse, they become as nervous as I am, so that after a while I get over it. Then we can have a normal conversation.'

This shyness manifested itself on train journeys. Lord Berners hated having to share a carriage and took elaborate precautions to maintain his privacy. Whenever the train stopped at a station, he would lower the window, wearing a black skull cap and dark glasses, beckoning fellow-travellers to join him. If that wasn't enough to ensure his solitude as far as the next stop, he would produce a large clinical thermometer with which he used to take his temperature with mounting anxiety every five minutes.

For all this he wasn't without a sense of mischief. He used to collect other people's calling cards and once selected those of the most notorious bores in London to send to a couple who were then honeymooning in the house he'd lent them in Rome, with the result that they spent their first days of married life devising complicated strategies to keep out of the way of their uninvited guests.

The twelfth Duke of St Albans, Osborne de Vere Beauclerk, was somewhat more gregarious. At the age of eighty-three he set off to America by freighter, travelled across the United States on a Greyhound bus and then went on a tour of Latin America, travelling second class all the way.

Travel was one thing, etiquette was quite a different matter. And where he was relaxed about the former, he was rigid in matters concerning the latter. A man inspecting the fire extinguishers was astonished one day to be told by his grace to take his wife's place at lunch because she hadn't arrived on time. When the Duchess finally made her appearance her husband refused to let her sit at the table.

Among the other duties expected of the hall porter at Brooks's, the Duke always got him to wind his

TRIALS OF A COUNTRY SEAT

'Excuse me! Is this anybody's seat?'

watch. And when he suggested attending the Queen's coronation in his capacity as Grand Falconer, complete with live falcon, and had the idea rejected in favour of a stuffed bird of prey, he chose to boycott the service completely.

A fellow-member of Brooks's was the Hon. John Denzil Fox Strangways, who was also a member of White's across the road. On the night of 24 January 1951 he was enjoying a drink in the bar at White's when he heard that the Labour cabinet minister

POCKET CARTOON
by OSBERT LANCASTER

ATHENÆUM

"Have a care, Fontwater! —we're not in White's!"

Aneurin Bevan was on the steps of the club, having dined with the Chief of the Air Staff. Leaving his drink and forgetting the war wound that had left him with a

game leg, Fox Strangways limped out of the bar to give
Bevan a kick on the posterior. Four days afterwards he
sent the White's committee his resignation.

On his death ten years later his will included
bequests of £1,000 to the hall porter at Brooks's, £500
to that club's steward and £250 to its night porter.

There's a certain remoteness of manner that haunts
centres of higher learning which itself can be pretty
unnerving for anyone who isn't prepared for it. When
C.S. Lewis was up for a fellowship at Magdalen,
Oxford, he went through the ritual of dining with the
college's governing body, and was seated next to the
elderly and awe-inspiring President, Sir Herbert
Warren. Not a word passed between them during the
first two courses. Only when the meat was served did
the President venture to ask the prospective candidate
for the English fellowship, 'Do you like poetry, Mr
Lewis?'

'Yes, President, I do,' Lewis replied, hoping this
might lead to a rather fuller exchange of ideas. But he
was wrong and as his neighbour seemed finished with
that topic of conversation he volunteered, 'I also like
prose.'

That elicited no response either and the two men
passed the rest of the meal without another word to
each other. Still, Lewis got his fellowship.

When it comes to assessing priorities in life, men
who have never known want manage to reflect some
curious predilections, typified by the Peer who
expressed an extraordinary attachment to his tummy-
button during the course of after-dinner conversation.
He and his companions had been discussing the
simplification of life and those things without which
existence would be impossible. According to this chap,

the one thing he couldn't do without was his navel. His friends asked for clarification. 'Well, whenever I have any free time,' he told them, 'I like to lie on my back and eat celery. Without my navel I should have nowhere to put the salt.'

His attitude simply reflected a different set of values from those of lesser mortals and it must be this factor which makes the behaviour of so many of the upper

classes virtually incomprehensible to everyone else. At best they give the impression of working on a different wavelength. But then history and tradition have a lot to answer for.

A venerable country squire who used to spend his summer afternoons happily ensconced in a garden chair by the front door of his seventeenth-century manor, selling tickets and postcards to day-trippers, was found by a couple of visitors snoozing peacefully under his panama hat when they stopped to have a look round.

'How long have you been here?' asked the husband benignly as he paid the entrance fee.

'Three hundred and seventy-eight years,' said the owner, pocketing the cash and settling down to sleep again.

UPPER
CRUST
AND
LOWER
ORDERS

'GOOD BREEDING,' SUGGESTED MARK TWAIN, 'CONSISTS in concealing how much we think of ourselves and how little we think of the other person.' No doubt he would have agreed that the reverse might show social position – but that that's not the same thing. Experience certainly bears that out when you consider some of the remarkable attitudes voiced by people who are clearly fairly near the top of the heap about those who aren't.

In the immediate post-war years, when rationing was still a part of everyday life, a letter appeared in *Picture Post* decrying the switching of emphasis in the milk ration to what the writer classified as 'the working classes'. In an ecstasy of bigotry he, or she, saw this as the first shot in a class war, claiming that the milk had been diverted to the poorer members of the community, not because they needed it, 'but to starve the better classes to whom it has always been a great item of food, thus the evil common man hopes to rid the country of the better classes in time.'

Another vitriolic correspondent, this time to the *Daily Express*, felt able to comment: 'Man is the lowest of the animals, especially those of the so-called working class.'

And a third decried the fact that dustmen were earning ten guineas a week, exclaiming in outrage, 'Even people with brains cannot earn that.'

Fortunately such extreme opinions represent the views of only a handful of unenlightened individuals. In

**'Burn the lot, Jeeves. I've been having talks with trade
union officials all day.'**

the majority of cases the tell-tale slips of social
distinction are milder and in many instances probably
quite unintentional.

When new police headquarters were opened in East
Grinstead it was soon noticed that the lavatories
carried their own specific designations. Those intended
for the use of magistrates were marked Ladies and
Gentleman. Members of the general public were
expected to use the loos marked Men and Women.
But the staff were allocated the ones bearing the
headings Male and Female.

That recalls the story of the army recruit who
reported to the MO one morning with tummy ache.

'What's the trouble,' he was asked.

'I've got a pain in my abdomen, sir.'

'Now listen, private,' said the doctor. 'Abdomens are for officers. NCOs have stomachs. What you've got is a pain in your belly.'

From the Senior Service comes a stores list in the same tradition:

Pots – Chamber – plain
Pots – Chamber – with Admiralty monogram in Blue, for hospital use
Pots – Chamber – fluted, with royal cipher in gold, for flag officers only
Pots – Chamber – round, rubber, lunatic.

At one time the cleansing department of Manchester City Council had three categories for the households from which it collected refuse: working class, middle class and better class.

While a woman in London who went into a large department store in the West End to ask for a maternity belt was told, 'We don't have nothing like that ... we do a more exclusive trade here. A better type of customer.'

Advertisements frequently betray similar sentiments. A firm of City solicitors on the lookout for a Conveyancing Manager let slip the fact that among their clients the successful candidate would have to be prepared to work with 'property speculators'.

There was a charity that placed an ad in *The Times* for a 'Blue-blooded girl desperately needed by well-known charity to pose for pin-up poster ultimately being seen by millions. Must be attractive and named in Debrett.'

In personal ads the discrimination can be even more blatant, if examples like these are anything to go by:

Superior widow would like a gentleman for companion, with motor preferred; farmer, if not a man.

Kentish Express

Young lady (26) desires refined Gentleman friend (27–30), or RAF.

Bristol Evening Post

A brace of gentlemen needed for Onslow Square flat; must be public school, English, Tory and heterosexual.

The Times

Though there is the risk you run if you fail to make it clear to the world at large that you were born with a silver spoon in your mouth – even one that was Sheffield plated. 'I strongly object to being described as "a woman",' wrote a highly indignant reader of the *Caterham and Warlingham Times*. 'When used by newspaper reporters, this term has a certain stigma attached to it. I am a young lady, well educated and refined and a highbrow of the first order.'

Closely linked with attitudes like these is the quality of what you might call tunnel vision that colours so many pronouncements made by one social group about another.

Faced with wartime shortages it was the better off who, according to some accounts, were having greater difficulty in coping with the situation than working-class housewives. Among the principal complaints was

Mistress *Did you water the ferns in the drawing room, Norah?*
Norah *Yes, mum. Can't you hear the water dripping on the carpet?*

the problem they faced in not being able to telephone and get what they wanted.

That does not mean that the lot of the working woman went unappreciated. After the war a correspondent to the *Western Mail*, who admitted that he never queued for anything during the war itself, came to a sharp understanding of what the majority of the nation's housewives must have gone through when he had to stand 'for an hour in a queue three deep, of first-class passengers, to reserve my table in the restaurant'. It's just that this particular gentleman and many like him lacked a certain amount of imagination.

The same could be said of the investor fifty years ago who reacted to the news that certain sections of the railway unions were contemplating a strike in August by writing to the *St Ives Times*: 'They know that shareholders in railways, already paying reduced dividends, depend on the summer season, yet they take this time of year for their ultimatum.

'Strikes should come under the heading of treason.'

Or there was Lord Shaftesbury who entered into the debate aroused in Wimborne St Giles, Dorset, over the difficulties experienced by the wife of the village bobby in drawing water from the well attached to the police house. 'I think that for the future welfare of the rising generation we should find women who are strong enough to draw water,' he argued with rather questionable logic. Because of the present incumbent's shortcomings he urged that the constable should be transferred to another post. 'Give us a constable whose wife will draw water,' demanded the earl.

The writer and critic Edward Sackville-West may have been less trenchant in his views on lesser mortals but his ideas were no more realistic. Inheriting Knole with its vast estate must have distanced him considerably from the tenor of normal life.

On being told that a friend had acquired a dog his only reply was, 'But how can he? He hasn't got a park to exercise it in.'

Sir Osbert Sitwell's father was cast in the same mould. His son recalled him staring out of a window at Renishaw Hall, looking far into the distance and commenting, 'Of course, there's absolutely no one between us and the Locker-Lampsons.' The fact that he was gazing over one of the most densely populated parts of the country had totally escaped him.

Similarly unseeing must have been the speaker who confidently informed his audience, 'In England there are no real class distinctions . . . people who are born in the East End do not always live there. They move to Cricklewood or Brighton.'

With views like these about it's hardly surprising that a 'Brain's Trust' panellist of Socialist sympathies was able to define 'upper crust' unhesitatingly as: 'A lot of crumbs held together with dough.'

Another area in which those who feel themselves superior are inclined to give themselves away is in their liberal dispensing of advice to people who haven't asked for it, and who would cheerfully tell them what to do with it, given half a chance. At one time the Ratcliffe Public Baths in Stepney carried a notice which read:

> The Council, with a view to extending the benefits of the baths, earnestly request you to recommend your friends and neighbours to use them. A bath once or twice a week promotes health, and contributes greatly to the well-being of the industrial classes.

However, the moment this laudable approach to public health posed a threat to the better off in the community the enthusiasm for it waned. A prolonged period of drought led to accusations of wastage from one water board, and encouraged a member of the senior management to suggest the situation might be eased if working people took one bath a fortnight instead of one a week!

Concern for public well-being, this time a question of moral welfare, was expressed by the Doncaster Free

Church Council before the war when it sent a letter of protest to the city's Carnival Committee about the proposed inclusion of Lady Godiva in the procession. 'We feel that the show will appeal to the animal instincts of the lower classes and fill the streets with vulgar sightseers,' the letter claimed.

Listeners to the BBC were seldom short of advice on what was good or bad for the rest of the audience. When a schools broadcast during a general election campaign inadvertantly carried a history programme on the Peasant's Revolt, at least one person who heard it accused the Corporation of being partial, and went as far as saying that the programme gave a lesson in 'class hatred'.

No doubt aware of its influence on public opinion, especially in its early days, the BBC has been known to go to great lengths to ensure that no one can accuse it of impropriety. The Abdication was a case in point. The Saturday following the king's departure from the throne Ambrose's late-night programme was carefully vetted to make sure that none of the titles of pieces of music played could be construed as a reflection on the national crisis. As a result numbers such as 'I Don't Want to Get Hot', 'We Go Well Together' and 'No Regrets' were removed from the programme. As a further precaution, the BBC imposed a general ban on 'Front-Page News'.

The Church hasn't been above giving advice as well as succour to the poor. Challenging the assertion made in one daily paper that there were thirteen and a half million underfed people in this country, the Bishop of St Edmundsbury and Ipswich in the late 1930s commented: 'The number who are underfed is really extremely small, and for the most part it is their own fault, because their money is unwisely spent.'

A quarter of a century later a similarly caring comment on housing subsidies was made by a London ratepayer to the *Barnes and Mortlake Herald* who put forward the idea that 'All council tenants could repay the subsidy by doing spare-time work for the ratepayers. Such things as street cleaning, tending our open spaces, supervising public conveniences and assisting in our libraries, offer scope for this.'

Perhaps the finest example of misplaced advice or guidance used to be found in Bedford prison, which at one time possessed an old edition of *Debrett* to help the prisoners while away lonely hours in their cells.

You can't beat war though for breaking down social barriers. One commentator during the last war came across a vivid example of democracy inherent in the British Army by watching soldiers ordering drinks at a bar. First he saw a couple of privates whom he identified as well-to-do men by the way they spoke and the fact that they ordered large whiskies 'at the new price'.

Next came a second-lieutenant. He asked for a gin and French.

Finally a major arrived, bustling up to the bar and asking the bar-maid for 'Half-pint of bitter, Miss.' This he downed in a gulp before bustling out again. Rank knew no prejudice – in uniform at any rate. It was only in civvy street that the cracks in this Model Army might have started to show.

In the RAF there was apparently an important distinction drawn between the wives of commissioned and non-commissioned men. Officers' wives were officially designated as 'ladies' but the wives of airmen were described as plain 'women'. This worried the correspondent to *Pearson's Weekly* who signed a letter on the subject 'Indignant' and asked whether the wife of an airman who worked his way up through the ranks and eventually gained a commission would automatically become a 'lady'.

I'll leave the last word on changes in the social order to Barbara Cartland, who entered the fringes of royal circles in 1981 when Lady Diana Spencer, her daughter's stepdaughter, married the Prince of Wales. During the course of an interview on the 'Today' programme, Miss Cartland was asked by Sandra Harris if she thought that traditional class barriers in Britain had broken down. 'Of course they have,' said Miss Cartland, 'or I wouldn't be sitting here talking to someone like you.'